Haldimand History

Crime and Punishment
1850-1950

by Cheryl MacDonald

Heronwood Enterprises

Care has been taken to trace the ownership of copyright material, including photographs, used in this book. The editor and publisher will welcome any information enabling them to rectify any reference or credit in subsequent editions.

Design and production: Heronwood Enterprises
Printing: Morris Printing Services Inc., Simcoe, Ontario

Front cover photo: Cayuga Court House and Jail by James G. McKay, from *Canadian Illustrated News*, 23 September 1876. (National Archives). Background is the existing stone wall surrounding the county jail (Cheryl MacDonald).

Published by
Heronwood Enterprises
R.R. 2, Nanticoke, Ontario, N0A 1L0
www.heronwoodent.ca

National Library of Canada Cataloguing in Publication
MacDonald, Cheryl E. (Cheryl Emily), 1952-
Haldimand History: Crime and Punishment 1850-1950
by Cheryl MacDonald

ISBN 0-9694896-4-1

Contents

Another murder. There is something really appalling in thus week after week having to record some deed of crime and bloodshed. Only a few weeks ago the whole country was shocked at the murder of Mr. Nellis, a highly respectable inhabitant of Haldimand; and while the atrocity of the deed was yet uppermost in the mind of the community, Mr. Roberts, a constable of Port Robinson was instantly shot dead in the streets of that village. ... The frequency and boldness of those dreadful outrages done in our midst, induces a painful watchfulness: law and authority appear set at defiance, and thus far justice deprived of her rights; life and prosperity has little protection, and we are pained to say the time has come, when for the sake of self-defence, the traveller through a section of Upper Canada deems it provident to go armed.

Haldimand Tribune
5 December 1854

Introduction

Crime has been with us from the beginning of time. Eve stole that forbidden apple. Her son Cain murdered his brother. The Bible, like the sacred writings of almost every culture, is full of crime stories.

There is nothing inherently glamorous about crime, which can bring terrible suffering to its victims and their families and serious consequences to its perpetrators. Often enough, crimes are driven by nothing more than stupidity, a complete lack of understanding about the consequences of certain actions. Sometimes, though, the impulses that lead to crime arise from more powerful sources, including hatred, jealousy and greed. Since these are emotions we have all experienced, in our imaginations we are usually able to cross the gulf that separates law-abiding citizens from law-breakers.

But is gulf the right metaphor for whatever separates law-breakers from the rest of society? Probably not. Crime may be more a matter of degree, a spectrum where acceptable behaviour blends almost seamlessly into illegal action. The case of John and James Young illustrates this. The uncle-and-nephew team were Victorian bully-boys, punks acting out their own version of contemporary machismo until they went a little too far and found themselves in the shadow of the gallows. Similarly, the case of Andrew Hannah is one of degree. He went a little too far in his attempt to settle a dispute with a neighbour and paid for it with a lengthy prison term.

At some level, most of us are able to recognize that there are only a few degrees of separation between ourselves and those who commit serious crimes. It is that recognition which makes true crime endlessly fascinating.

This book contains some of the most interesting crime stories from Haldimand County history. Most are serious crimes, usually murder or manslaughter. In the past, as now, the most serious crimes usually attracted the most attention, resulting in extensive newspaper coverage. The details contained in historic newspaper reports provide plenty of insight into the crimes themselves. But newspaper reports also provide something more: information on the everyday life of ordinary people that might not otherwise have come to light.

Haldimand History: Crime and Punishment offers a brief glimpse into one aspect of the county's past. Much more could be written on the topic—stories of later crimes, details about the courts and the individuals who served them. For now, this book provides some insight into a colorful aspect of our history, one that is as much as part of our heritage as the historic buildings which are part of the landscape.

Cheryl MacDonald
Heronwood, October 2004

Acknowledgements

For more than twenty years I have been collecting information on crime and punishment in Haldimand and Norfolk Counties. So many people have helped by recalling sensational crimes, suggesting areas of research, sharing documents, or providing enthusiastic encouragement, that it would be impossible to name them all. For this book, however, I would like especially thank the following: John Ayre; Jeff Balin; John Burtniak; Lori Chambers; Dunnville District Heritage Association; Allison (Sam) Gowling; Margaret Houghton, Special Collections, Hamilton Public Library; Library and Archives Canada; Mary Nelles; Jennifer Tigert, Haldimand County Museum; Barbra Lang Walker, former curator, Edinburgh Square Heritage and Cultural Centre; Eva Brook Donly Museum, Simcoe; and McMaster University.

Thanks also go to the staff of the Nanticoke post office and Morris Printing, Simcoe, who provide invaluable support services. Finally, I would like to thank my family, especially my sister, Sandra, for their love and encouragement.

Author's Note:
Through much of its history, the Haldimand County Jail was referred to as the county "gaol". As this old English spelling of the word is now considered obsolete, I have opted for the more modern spelling, "jail". However, I have given the spelling exactly as it appears in historic documents, which may or may not have used "gaol" and frequently misspelled the word as "goal".

Chapter One

The Notorious Townsend Gang

In mid-October 1854, residents of western Haldimand and eastern Norfolk counties were victims of an extended crime spree. A gang of five young men in their late teens and early twenties moved eastward along the stage road [Highway 3], robbing stores and travellers. One of the victims was Thomas Graham, owner of a store and tavern in Walpole Township, who was robbed of $12. At another store, one of the thieves grabbed the proprietor, Mr. Husband, by the hair and pulled him over the counter while others took £20 from the money drawer. A little further down the road they took $6 from William Downs. They also stopped team drivers along the highway and demanded cash.

Around 8:30 on the evening of October 18 Willliam Townsend, John Blowes, George King, William Bryson and John Lettice reached the home and business establishment of John Hamilton Nelles. William Townsend, the leader of the gang, rapped at the door, demanding to be let in. Everyone else in the household was in bed at the time, although not all were asleep. Lucy Humphrey, Nelles' sister-in-law, later testified that she heard someone shout, "Open the door or I'll blow you through!"[1] Then shots rang out. John Hamilton Nelles staggered across the sitting-room, crying that he was shot, and collapsed on the carpet.

Augustus Nelles, brother of John, claimed three of the robbers were wearing black hats. One man was wearing a white hat and also had a dark moustache, which according to Augustus, looked fake. The mustachioed man—who apparently was William Townsend — along with at least one companion entered. The rest of them waited outside the building. Meanwhile, Mrs. Nelles and her sister-in-law Lucy Humphrey emerged from a bedroom. When the men demanded money, Lucy responded that she didn't know where it was kept, but Mrs. Nelles pointed to the bedroom. While the three robbers ransacked the room Mrs. Nelles escaped through a window and ran to a neighbour's, but before Lucy could escape one of the gang came back into the room with her.

Within five minutes, the Townsend gang was on the road again, with nothing to show for their latest crime but a gold watch. As soon as they were gone, the Nelles family sent for a doctor. When Dr. Henry Whicher arrived, he found that John Hamilton Nelles had three bullet wounds in the left chest. Nelles lingered until midnight, complaining of pains in his back, then died.

Meanwhile, the robbers headed towards Cayuga, stopping at George Gibson's tavern, where they persuaded Gibson to drive them by wagon to Cayuga Station. Townsend also stopped briefly at the home of his mother to tell her that he was leaving and would not return for several years. Soon afterwards, the robbers boarded a Buffalo, Brantford and Goderich Railroad train. Once in the U.S., they went their separate ways.

Authorities got word of the murder and robbery early on the morning of October 19th. According to Haldimand County high constable Peter Campbell, the news arrived around 8 a.m.

> I... prepared to follow to follow the murderers without delay. I found plenty of men ready and willing to assist me in the pursuit. I selected five, and we proceeded to the Cayuga Station. Here Robt. Flanders joined our company, and we went by the next train to Buffalo.[2]

Because several of the posse members knew the suspects, it was assumed there would be little difficulty identifying them and taking them into custody. To provide further assistance, friends of John Nelles quickly posted a $100 reward.[3]

From the information they were able to piece together, law enforcement officials suspected William Townsend, Garrett Patterson and George Morrison, all of whom had run afoul of the law at some point or other.

The shooting of John Hamilton Nelles

On October 21, Patterson was arrested in Hamilton. Although he was a known associate of William Townsend, several people claimed to have seen him in a Methodist church around the time of the murder, and eventually it became clear that he had not participated in the murder of John Nelles.

The whereabouts of Lettice and Townsend at this time are unknown, but Blowes had gone to Galt, where he found work as a stage driver. After quitting his job on November 30, he headed back to Hamilton, where he was arrested on December 11 at a "house of ill-fame" kept by a woman known as Limping Jenny. Along with constables from Brantford and Hamilton, Robert Flanders of Canfield was involved in the arrest.[4]

George King worked as a brakeman on the Great Western Railway for a period of time, then joined a saddler named James Smith. Together they planned to rob a bank in Cobourg. Although these plans failed, they did rob a jeweller's shop in that town on December 4th, carrying off five silver watches, 200 rings, 11 gold lockets and three gold chains, which they buried in Yorkville, near Toronto. King and Smith then proceeded to Hamilton, where they joined up with two other young criminals. They robbed several unwary travellers before being captured by a group of Saltfleet farmers on December 18.

William Bryson was also arrested. Bryson, King and Blowes spent the winter in the Haldimand County Jail, Cayuga, awaiting the spring assizes.

On Friday, April 13, 1855, George King, John Blowes and William Bryson went to trial at the Cayuga courthouse. Then, as now, murder trials aroused a great deal of curiosity and the courtroom was crowded. Among the observers was Thomas Messenger, one of Haldimand's first newspaper publishers, who subsequently printed a pamphlet on the trial and its aftermath. He described two of the accused in some detail.

George King was born in Suffolk, England and came to Canada as a child. A handsome young man, he had been brought up in the British Wesleyan Church and "regularly sent to school for about eleven or twelve years."[5] In late 1853 he went to work, first on the railway, then as a stagecoach driver. According to Messenger, "It was at this time that he first departed from the path of virtue and rectitude; and that, in consequence of meeting and associating with men already hardened in crime, who induced him to frequent houses of ill fame." [6] Spending his money on drink and gambling left King chronically short of money, and he soon turned to crime.

John Blowes was born in Flamborough Township in 1836, the son of respectable Anglicans. In contrast to the good-looking King, Blowes had "a low thick forehead ... small sluggish eyes ... thick neck, heavy drowsy expression of countenance" and a "stupid smile." According to Messenger, "He seemed above fear, or rather too morbid in sense to feel or shun it."[7] Possibly he was mentally defective.Messenger provided little information about Bryson, who was from the Niagara area, where his father had been a labourer.

All three young men entered a plea of not guilty before Judge McLean. They contended that since none of them had been in the Nelles house when the shooting took place they had not committed murder. But, as Judge McLean pointed out in his charge to the jury, the gang had

> banded together for the purpose of robbing and appropriating to their own use the goods of others, without the shadow of right, and ... armed themselves with pistols, dirks, bowie knives &c., for the purpose of defending themselves against the officers of the law, or of enforcing their demands upon such persons as they should see fit to rob.[8]

The jurors, men of property like most of the gang's victims, took 15 minutes to render a verdict of guilty.

Sentence was pronounced the next day. Blowes, King and Bryson were placed in the dock. Bryson, the youngest, stood in front, his face flushed. His mother, heavily veiled in black, sat nearby, until the sheriff escorted her to his office to so that she would not have to hear her son sentenced.

King was "pale and trembling" and at one point "buried his face in his hands."[9] Blowes, impervious to the emotion and drama of the moment, smiled at those around him. Judge McLean asked each prisoner to make a statement. Both King and Bryson said they were not guilty of murder. Blowes only smiled. The judge then reviewed the crime and legal precedents and sentenced all three to hang on May 18th.

Before the date arrived, Bryson's sentence was commuted to life imprisonment. Because of his youth, it was felt, he was more easily influenced by bad companions and so deserved mercy. In the meantime, King and Blowes were comforted by clergymen, Blowes by Anglican priest Bold Cudmore Hill, King by a Methodist minister, Mr. Vining.

Religion was very much a part of daily Victorian life, including the justice system. During their final days, the condemned men were expected to make peace with God, and confessions signed by each of them on May 17th suggest they had done so. "I acknowledge the justice of my sentence, and forgive all my enemies" King stated in his confession. "I earnestly hope that God will, in his infinite goodness, pardon all my sins, and receive my poor soul for the merits and sake of my gracious Saviour Jesus Christ."[10]

Blowes, who could not write, made his mark on a statement that was probably drafted by Reverend Hill:

> I acknowledge the justice of my sentence, in the eyes of God and man, and I wish to die in peace with all mankind. I freely, from the bottom of my heart, forgive all my enemies, and I humbly hope all my fellow-creatures, whom I have wronged or injured, will forgive me. I trust and hope that God will graciously look

> upon me in mercy and pity, and pardon all my sins and transgressions.[11]

Once the confessions were signed, there was nothing to do but wait to be led to the gallows.

Public executions were still the norm in Canada West in 1855. One of the reasons was that legislators believed it was important that justice be seen to be done. And so a scaffold was erected outside the front entrance of the Haldimand County Courthouse. On the day of the executions, hundreds gathered to watch the proceedings and a holiday atmosphere prevailed. Men pitched coppers and placed wagers, sold various items and set off firecrackers. There was also plenty of drinking and cursing, according to one reporter. "I never witnessed so much intoxication, even on a holiday, as there was at Cayuga."[12]

Around 1 p.m., King and Blowes were led from their cells, accompanied by two clergymen, the county sheriff, and several constables. The shackles of the condemned men were removed, and they walked to the scaffold "with firm steps."[13] Each made a brief speech, the gist of which was a statement of faith in the hereafter and a warning to avoid bad company. Then the hangman pulled black hoods over their faces.

According to the *Brant Herald*, the trap door of the scaffold suddenly gave way at this point, prolonging the anxiety King and Blowes must have been feeling. A few moments later, all was ready. The young men were placed on the trap door, nooses placed around their necks, and the trap opened.

King died instantly of a broken neck. Despite the hangman's efforts, Blowes convulsed for several minutes, a situation Messenger attributed to the unusual thickness of his neck. Somehow, the *Brantford Expositor* reported, the hood was torn away, revealing his contorted face. Although the hangman "shuddered at the spectacle and drew himself away in loathing," the women in the crowd surged forward for a better look, especially after a constable shouted from the scaffold, "Stand back and give the ladies a chance to see."[14] Some of the women were carrying young children in their arms.

The execution of Townsend gang members George King and John Blowes.

The bodies of King and Blowes hung on the scaffold until about 3 p.m., then were cut down. King's body was taken to Yorkville by members of his family. One source suggests Blowes might have been taken to Dundas, but Thomas Messenger stated that his stepfather could not afford to pay for the transportation and burial.

Meanwhile, two members of the Townsend gang remained at large. John Lettice, according to tradition, was shot while fleeing from the scene of another crime. Townsend remained free for several months. Then, in August 1855, rumours reached Haldimand County that a man answering Townsend's description was living near Rock Island, Illinois. Robert Flanders, still a county constable, went after him. The suspect was apparently working in travelling sideshows in the American midwest and Flanders followed him through a couple of towns before catching up with him and positively identifying him. In the meantime, however, the Rock Island sheriff had told the owner of the circus in confidence about the suspicions surrounding one of his employees. Unable to keep the secret, the circus owner had passed the information on to the ringmaster, and eventually word got to the suspect. Before Flanders could arrange for his arrest he disappeared.

Another two years passed. Finally, in 1857 a man thought to be William Townsend was arrested in the U.S. and extradited to Canada to stand trial for the murder of Nelles. The trial began on Thursday, September 24, at the Haldimand County Courthouse. Justice Burns presided, with Solicitor-General Henry Smith serving as Crown prosecutor and S.B. Freeman of Hamilton conducting the defence.[15] The jury included James Lindsay, Nanticoke; William Hare, Rainham; Alexander Lamond, Seneca; Harlo H. Johnson, Dunnville; William Ross, Seneca; William Dukesberry, Oneida; Samuel Hodges, Canborough; James Gillespie, Oneida; Peter Drake, Dunnville; Thomas Woodside, Dunnville; William Hopkins, Cayuga; and L.H. Michener, Moulton.[16]

The defendant swore he was Robert J. McHenry, a Scot from the Glasgow area who had emigrated to the United States around 1837. Because photography was still in its infancy and fingerprinting was unknown to police forces, the initial focus of the trial was to determine whether or not McHenry was lying. According to the *Grand River Sachem*, "There were 36 witnesses for the Crown, most of whom swore *positively* to Townsend's identity, and 54 for the defence, who were equally *positive* that he was not that notorious rascal."[17]

Although they could not agree on the identity of the man in the dock, the various witnesses presented a great deal of information about William Townsend, as well as details about working-class life in 1850s Ontario. Townsend was born in Black Rock [Buffalo] on August 7, 1832. His father was a carpenter and joiner who moved around a bit and at one time worked in Port Dalhousie. Eventually, he settled on a farm near Canfield.

By the time William Townsend was in his early teens, his father had died. Although his mother would later marry David Dewar, young William was forced to support himself. Like many young men of the time, one of the occupations he turned to was farm labour. Some farm labourers worked mainly for one farmer, but others travelled about from place to place, helping out at planting and harvest time. When no farm work was available, they had to look for other jobs. Townsend was one of these. He probably started out working for neighbours. However, by 1846, he was working aboard the *Mohawk,* a government steamer. Martha Stewart, the girlfriend of one of the ship's officers, testified that Townsend was "a good boy"[18] and that he saw service in Dunnville, Port Maitland and Penetanguishene. But other testimony revealed that he stole a boat from the *Mohawk* and sold it in Dunnville for $5. Then, around 1848, he deserted.

By this time he had acquired a couple of tattoos on his wrist — his initials, W.T., and a small anchor. His ears had also been pierced. Many people described him as a quiet man, almost morose, and noted that he did not drink liquor, although he was known to treat friends and colleagues in the taverns he frequented.

After leaving the *Mohawk*, Townsend tried various odd jobs. He worked on rafts and boats along the Welland Canal. From time to time he went back to farm work. At one point he was employed by Martin Knowles in Haldimand County. On another occasion, he worked at George Robinson's farm in Seneca Township, where he was engaged in harvesting, raking and binding. He also showed up at other farms for at least one barn-raising and one work bee.

For a time Townsend worked at a North Cayuga sawmill as a fireman. His main responsibility there was to keep the fire going in order to provide the steam that powered the mill's equipment. One of the mill's owners, the Reverend Mr. Haw, testified that Townsend already had such a bad reputation that he put his household on alert. Apparently Haw was about to receive a quantity of cash and Townsend was asking a lot of questions about it.

Around 1851, Townsend tried to learn the cooper's trade but lacked either the talent or the dedication needed. Although he worked at different coopers' shops in Dunnville and the

Niagara Peninsula, at least two witnesses noted that he was not very skilled. One employer fired him after he had made just a few barrels. Townsend also worked for a time helping with the construction of Dunnville's new town hall, and one witness claimed he drove a cab in Hamilton around 1853.

When he was not working at respectable employment, Townsend was usually engaged in one of two activities. He was a talented mimic noted for his female impersonations and black-face minstrel shows. With others he travelled to various communities, including Caledonia, Dunnville, Merritville and Marshville, putting on performances. Perhaps performing really was Townsend's forte. On the other hand, it might have been a cover for criminal activities. As several witnesses revealed, Townsend frequently turned to crime, working as a pickpocket and highwayman between more respectable jobs. Ultimately, his penchant for crime would lead to the murder of John Hamilton Nelles.

But was the man who claimed to be R. McHenry really William Townsend? Witnesses could not agree on the colour of Townsend's eyes and hair, whether or not his eyebrows joined, or other distinguishing features. A long parade of witnesses discussed Townsend's colouring, the shape of his face, scars he was supposed to have on his left brow and one ankle, his unusually large and misshapen toes, which were apparent even when he wore boots. About the only things they agreed upon was that he was dark-haired, resembled his sisters and had a gift for mimicry.

One witness, Peter Schram, said, "Townsend had a low forehead, black hair, heavy eyebrows running quite across, high cheek bones, a short nose, thin lips, a small black eye, a short chin, dark complexion and a flat face."[19] But another man recalled, "He had dark brown hair and dark hazel eyes. His forehead was tolerably wide, his eyes sunk and his cheeks hollow."[20] Even William Bryson, who had been sent to prison for his part in Nelles' murder, was unable to make a positive identification. Bryson had been brought to Cayuga from Kingston penitentiary to identify McHenry and to testify in court. At first glance he thought the accused was not Townsend. Part of the problem was that McHenry was wearing a full beard. However, during the second day of the trial, the solicitor-general insisted that the defendant be shaved. At first McHenry resisted, then gave in, and Bryson identified him positively as William Townsend.

Who was this man? William Townsend? Or Robert J. McHenry?

There were suspicions that Bryson hoped to earn a reduced sentence with his testimony, although he denied this under oath. Equally suspect was the testimony of Townsend's family, including his mother, stepfather David Dewar, and sisters Elizabeth and Frances. All denied that the prisoner was William Townsend. So did Elizabeth's father-in-law, Ezra Smith of Canborough. Freely admitting that he had known the Townsend family for some time, Smith stated he had "no sympathy for Townsend."[21] Nevertheless, he was adamant: the man in the dock was not the individual wanted by authorities.

While the courtroom drama unfolded, there were some problems behind the scenes. At the beginning of proceedings of Friday, September 25, Judge McLean addressed the jury. He had been informed that large bets were being placed on the outcome of the trial and that certain members of the jury were involved. The rumour proved true:

> A juryman then rose and said that there was one of their number who had asserted in his presence that he would take a bet that the prisoner was not Townsend. The juryman referred to said that he had made use of the expression, but he had not made any bet. If, however, it was objected to, he would rather not sit on

> the case. His Lordship observed that the offer was a very improper one, and no juryman should form, much less express, an opinion until the whole of the evidence had been adduced.[22]

There is no evidence that the anonymous jury member was removed.

The trial continued through Friday and into Saturday afternoon. Finally, at 3:30 the jury retired. Court was adjourned until 9 p.m., but did not resume until 10 when the judge mounted the bench and sent the sheriff to see how the jury was progressing. A short time later, William Hopkins of Cayuga entered the court room. He reported that the jury was unable to reach an agreement and had not even been able to appoint a foreman. Instead, Hopkins had been asked to serve as the spokesman for the jurors. He told the judge that one juror was undecided, seven were in favour of convicting the prisoner and the remaining four were sure he was innocent. "One of the jurors is said to have asserted that he would sit on his seat until he was carried out a corpse, rather than convict the prisoner."[23] Convinced that they would never reach a verdict, the judge discharged them. McHenry was sent back to jail to await a new trial at the spring assizes.

By the time April rolled around, authorities had decided that Townsend/McHenry could not get a fair trial in Haldimand County, so the venue was changed to Welland. Again, much of the testimony focused on the identity of the prisoner. Again, the evidence was so contradictory and uncertain that it seemed there would be a repeat of the Cayuga trial. But this time the jury rendered a verdict: McHenry was *not* William Townsend and should be set free.

The decision was controversial. A short time later, a petition was presented to the government, asking for yet another trial, this one in Haldimand County. But no such trial would ever take place. McHenry was set free and the murderer of John Hamilton Nelles never paid for his crime.

Chapter Two

Haldimand County Courthouse

When King and Blowes took their final walk to the gallows, the Haldimand County Courthouse was already a community symbol. In 1849, new legislation had changed the structure of Haldimand County. Up to that point, matters of justice and the day-to-day operations of the area had been mainly in the hands of district councils. In Haldimand's case, the Niagara District, London District, Gore District and Talbot District had, at various times, held jurisdiction over the county's townships. With the passing of the new law, Haldimand County Council was made responsible for municipal affairs, while the Haldimand County Court would dispense justice.

Although Cayuga barely deserved to be called a village in 1850, it was strategically located on the Talbot Road [Highway 3] which led from Niagara to the western part of the province. A bridge had been constructed where the road crossed the Grand River at Cayuga. A short distance upstream was an impressive hill offering a panoramic view of the river and surrounding landscape. This hill was chosen as the site of the courthouse.

By May 1850, the building plans had been drawn up. The man responsible for the design was Frederick W. Cumberland. Born in London, England in 1821, Cumberland arrived in Toronto in 1847 and formed a partnership with Thomas Ridout. Among the projects they tackled between 1850 and 1853 was the Church of the Ascension and the Central School in Hamilton, St. James Cathedral in Toronto and the Toronto post office. Cumberland's plan for the Haldimand courthouse called for a handsome building in the Classical Revival style, featuring a two-storey central block and one-storey wings on either side. In addition, a sturdy jail would be attached to the courthouse. Cumberland originally planned for both structures to be made of stone, but in order to save money certain changes were made. Part of the courthouse was built of brick with stone facings.

Almost from the beginning of construction there were difficulties, including political controversy. Some residents of Seneca and Oneida Townships were trying to secede from Haldimand and join with Wentworth County. It is difficult to determine just how widespread the support for this action was. However, David Thompson, Haldimand's parliamentary representative, made it clear that any change would be costly. Haldimand County Council had already spent a great deal on construction of the courthouse and jail.

That was in June 1850. Seven months later, in January 1851, the courthouse was still unfinished and problems with the structure and operating systems had been discovered. That month, Dr. John Jarron, reeve of Moulton and Sherbrooke presented a motion to county council. Seconded by Agnew P. Farrell, reeve of Dunn Township, it requested that architect Frederick Cumberland and W. Mills be contacted. The "hot air apparatus" that was supposed to heat the courthouse was not working properly. "Certain of the valves do not act, throwing out cold instead of hot air."[1] The motion also requested that Mills, a St. Catharines contractor, be refused payment until everything was finished to the council's satisfaction. The next month, councillors Robert Young and Robert Cook tabled a motion asking the county clerk to "notify the architect of the County Buildings at Cayuga that the walls are falling down, calling his immediate attention thereto, and to the leaky state of the roofs."[2] Council requested a full report by the next session.

The problems were apparently solved, at least for the time being. In May, council accepted a tender from William H. Pym for construction of a plank and picket fence around the jail.

Haldimand County Courthouse in 1873. Note the board fence surrounding the jail yard.

(The fence, which stood about eight feet high, would eventually become a major thorn in the side of Haldimand authorities.) In July, Cumberland himself came out to speak to council. Asked when the buildings would be completed, he promised to finish the work by the following week. The jail was also completed around the same time.

The problems that had been detected in the courthouse during construction did not go away. Around March 1865, when the grand jury reported on the conditions of the courthouse and jail, they noted that the "hot air apparatus for heating the premises is out of order." Even when it worked, the building was not well heated, and they recommended that the system be fixed before another winter. In addition, there were problems with waste disposal, as the grand jury reported:

> They would again call the attention of the County Council to the necessity of adopting some method for removing the soil accumulated in the cesspool used by the prisoners, which has been very offensive and which must be detrimental to the health of the prisoners as well as those County officers whose offices are situated in the county buildings.[3]

In 1884, the problem had still not been solved. After a visit on June 12, the inspector of prisons wrote:

> Bad odours were perceptible through the whole upper part of the gaol. On enquiry, this was found to proceed from a water-closet, which, though in the gaol building, is attached to the court-room, and is in daily use, without being properly ventilated or having a proper supply of water. It would be better that this closet should be kept closed, except during the sessions of court.[4]

Two more buildings were added to Courthouse Park in the 1870s. Inside the courthouse, storage for important documents, especially land registrations, was running out. As a result, a separate, fire-proof registry office was constructed. The tender was awarded to John McClure, with Samuel Jessop appointed supervisor of the construction. In 1877, a new house was built for the jailer, who, up to that time, had lived in the jailhouse.

Disaster struck just before Christmas 1922. Around 5:45 on the morning of December 20, jailer Thomas Walsh woke up to the smell of smoke. Investigating, he discovered the courthouse was on fire. He gave the alarm, woke his wife and their 4-year-old granddaughter, Marie, who was living with them at the time. They started carrying out household belongings. Meanwhile, Judge G.H. Hopkins, who was living in the 1870s jailer's residence at the time, also removed household items. Meanwhioe, two male prisoners were freed to help fight the fire. But the flames had taken hold. They destroyed the courthouse, numerous documents and the law association's library.

It was believed that the fire had either started in the furnace or in gas stoves that were left on in order to keep the water pipes from freezing. Possibly some of the courthouse could have been saved. Certainly Cayuga firefighters tried valiantly, but the water supply was inadequate and one of the fire hoses was in such poor condition that it was nearly useless.

The flames had barely died down when the *Dunnville Chronicle* made a suggestion which the *Haldimand Advocate* described as "an absurd proposal."[5] Why not move the

By the time Page's Atlas *was published in 1877, a jailer's house had been built beside the courthouse. Note the stone wall surrounding the jail yard.*

courthouse and the county administration to Dunnville? After all, Dunnville was still the biggest town in the county, with a population of about 3200. Cayuga had fewer than 800 residents. In addition, Dunnville had a modern fire department, dependable electricity, good sewers and, as soon as the new water system was completed, would have a steady supply of water. All the problems that plagued the courthouse and the firefighters could be solved.

The suggestion was not given serious consideration. Cayuga was still more centrally located than Dunnville. Furthermore, the registry office, jail and jailer's residence were still intact. County Council decided to rebuild on the same site. By April, Stuart Brothers of Hamilton was awarded the contract. The firm, which had built the Cayuga high school in 1921, estimated the cost of rebuilding the courthouse at around $100,000. The new design, prepared by Frank Barber and Associates of Toronto, called for a modern structure. Again, there wold be a central block with slightly smaller blocks on either side, but the domed cupola that been one of the outstanding features of the first courthouse was gone.

One new element was the inclusion of a scaffold within a few feet of the judge's bench. According to the *Hamilton Herald*, it was "built into the hallway just beside the door leading out into

Surveying the damage of the 1922 fire. L-R, *unknown, J. W. Sheppard, Judge G. H. Hopkins, J.C. Eccles, Sheriff Michael McConnell, Alex Mitchell.*

the jail exercise yard."[6] Most of the time it was out of sight—the main beam pulled back into the ceiling and was covered with a tin plate, just as a hole for a stovepipe might be. But prisoners had to pass by it on their way from their cells to the courthouse, and it was a grim reminder of the ultimate penalty imposed by Canadian law. According to the *Herald* article, members of the county council were "struck with horror at having so gruesome a thing for all time in their beautiful courthouse, but the Government inspector simply said to them, 'No scaffold, no courthouse—take your choice.'"[7]

The formal opening of the new courthouse took place on Wednesday, September 24, 1924. Before proceedings got under way, those in attendance were allowed to tour the building and comment on the new marble floors and impressive wood paneling. Then the ceremony began with County Warden George Montgomery in the chair. A number of speakers followed, including former MPP Thomas Marshall, MP Mark Senn and Harrison Arrell, who served as both county Crown attorney and county clerk. Former county wardens Weylie

Laying the cornerstone for the new courthouse, 1924.

Hudspeth, R.F. Miller and Dr. R.N. Berry, MPP also spoke, as did David Hastings, the publisher of the *Dunnville Gazette* who had once served as a police magistrate. Judge Charles Wesley Colter, who had served as Haldimand county judge twenty years earlier, traveled by train from his home in St. Thomas to take part in the ceremony. His remarks reflected the emotions of the day.

> Law, he said, must be administered in a dignified proper and just manner, and great credit is due to those who have provided these facilities in the splendid new courthouse. Public buildings should be not only commodious, but handsome and impressive, and in this respect Haldimand had a courthouse which would compare favorably with any in the Dominion. [8]

Haldimand's commodious, handsome and impressive new courthouse would serve the county into the next century.

Haldimand Court Officials 1850-1950

County Judges

Bernard Foley	March 1850 - December 1854
John Gusatvus Stevenson	February 1855 - April 1884
M.C. Upper	June 1884 - February 1893
D. MacMillan	March 1893 - January 1903
T.A. Snider[1]	February 1903 - July 1903
Charles Wesley Colter	July 1903 - May 1904
George B. Douglas	May 1904 - January 1915
John A. Murphy[2]	January 1915 - February 1915
A.T. Ecles[2]	June 1915 - April 1916
G.H. Hopkins	April 1916 - February 1932
W.S. West	March 1932 - November 1942
E.S. Livermore[2]	December 1942 - June 1943
Helen Kinnear	June 1943 - September 1962

County Crown Attorneys

John Gustavus Stevenson	1850 - 1855
Walter Graham	1855 - 1856
T.H. Aikman	1856 - 1867
John R. Martin	1867 - 1894
Charles Welsey Colter, K.C.	1894 - 1903
John A. Murphy	1903 - 1915
Harrison Arrell, K.C.	1915 -

County Sheriffs

Richard Martin	1850 (year appointed)
Robert H. Davis	1878 " "
Michael McConnell	1907 " "
Weylie S. Hudspeth	1927 " "
Robert F. Miller	1935 " "
B.L. Edgecombe	1950 " "

[1]Deputy County Judge

[2]Acting County Judge

Source: *Minutes and Auditor's Report of the County Council of the County of Haldimand for the Year 1950.*

Chapter Three

Jailbreak! John and James Young

On Saturday, November 20, 1875, Abel McDonald was on his way home from Hamilton. The Walpole Township farmer, then in his early thirties, had sold a load of barley to a Mr. Osborne for $35. As he followed the Plank Road south, the daylight faded. McDonald decided to stop in Caledonia and have something to eat and drink at Murphy's hotel.

At the hotel he fell into conversation with John Young, a 28-year-old carpenter. As they were having dinner together, the men were joined by John's 24-year-old nephew, James Young. James was annoyed with John and let him know it.

For the past few days, the two Youngs had been touring the area between Caledonia and Hamilton with a rented horse and buggy, stopping at various inns for a number of drinks. On Thursday, they were at Spohn's Hotel on Hamilton Beach. On Friday, they headed back up Hamilton mountain, stopping at Swayzie's Hotel for breakfast, then at Mason's Hotel. By noon, they were at McGee's hotel in Ryckman's Corners. The horse they were driving had been rented there, and when John found out he would have to pay for a full day's rental, he decided to keep the horse a while longer and head further south. He and James dropped by Patterson's Hotel in Mount Hope, then continued on to Caledonia to see Emily and Susan Barber.

The Youngs were precisely the kind of young men that respectable Victorians worried about. Earlier in the century, most young men either stayed on the family farm or worked alongside their craftsmen fathers in small workshops. Industrialization and the steady drift of young people to the city had changed this. Many young men were now able to earn

John Young

wages some distance from home, far away from the watchful eyes of their parents and neighbours. But few were able to find full-time employment, and in their idle hours an alarming number of them frequented bars, pool-rooms and other unsavory locations.

John Young was one of these men. At the age of 14, he started going to dances, saloons and gambling establishments. He also began keeping company with "the bad and disreputable class of women who are found in almost every city, town, village and country."[1] At 22 he was "compelled under certain circumstances to get married."[2] He and his wife lived at Ryckman's Corners, on Hamilton mountain, and apparently their son was born here. Although John felt deep affection for the young boy, his marriage soon fell apart, mostly because he continued to see other women. By the time he was 24, he was again living the life of a single man.

On Friday night, John and his nephew had called on the Barber girls, walked around the village for a few hours, then escorted them home and returned to Murphy's hotel. The next day, John and James drove around with Emily Barber for a short time in the morning, then returned to the hotel for lunch. After the meal, John said he was going out for a while but would return shortly so that they could drive the horse back to Ryckman's Corners before dark.

James waited for hours for his uncle to return. Finally, he knocked on the door of Mrs. Hill's house, where the Barber girls were staying. Emily informed him that John had gone back to the hotel. So, James went back to the hotel, found his uncle and gave him a piece of his mind.

James William Young

James ignored the stranger who was sitting with John. After the meal, John and Abel moved into the bar. Around 7 o'clock, McDonald and the hotel ostler, John Beatty, went out to the stable to look at cut on the leg of McDonald's horse. At that point, John and his nephew decided to call on the Barber girls again. On the way, John said to James, "I am going to make some money to-night."[3]

When James questioned him, John revealed his plan to rob Abel McDonald as he drove along the Plank Road. James thought it was a bad idea, but John told him there was no danger. When James still resisted, John called him a coward.

"I then asked him," James later recalled, "'what had got into his head to do such a thing.' He replied in 'consequence of being short of money, and that the whiskey had got into his head.'"[4] James said he had enough money to pay all their bills and get them home. But John would not be deterred.

What happened next is unclear. They reached the Barber home and James apparently went in for a few moments. Then he came out again and caught up to his uncle. Together they crossed the iron bridge across the Grand River. Although James would later say he still wanted no part of the robbery John was planning, John claimed that his nephew had already made up his mind to help him. John, possibly assisted by

Highway Robbery

Abel McDonald was not the only resident of Haldimand to fall victim to robbers as he travelled along the county roads. In November 1860, one "daring robbery" took place along the "river road" between Cayuga and Caledonia.

William Fitzgerald, a shoemaker, was travelling from Cayuga to Hamilton to buy some leather. He set out late at night in order to reach the city early in the morning. A little after midnight, when he was about a mile past York, two men suddenly appeared from behind some logs that had been piled on the side of the road. While one caught his horse, the other approached Fitzgerald and said, "You have a load of hides here; we will ease you of the money, and leave you the hides." The robber then put his hand in Fitzgerald's pocket and pulled out his pocketbook. Then the two men hurried away with the wallet, which contained $235 in cash.

Fitzgerald continued to Seneca village, reached it about 2 a.m. and reported the crime. However, because it was so dark he could give no description of the highwaymen. As the *Haldimand Tribune* reported on November 22, the men might well have been acquaintances who knew he was heading to Hamilton with a large sum of money. "The pocket-book, we learn, was picked up near Simms' lock, *minus* its contents, of course. No clue as yet has been found, which seems likely to lead to the detection of the offenders."

A similar incident led to an arrest in December 1864. On December 15, 1864, the *Haldimand Tribune* reported on Queen vs. Hill, a case heard before justice John G. Stevenson:

> The prisoner and Wm. Jones had been playing at a bowling saloon in Caledonia during the afternoon. Just before dark Jones started for home up the river and when opposite R. McKinnon's farm, about a mile above the bridge, prisoner seized his horse by the head and demanded his money. Jones offered $1 to prisoner to let him go, but the latter refused unless he gave up the whole in his possession. Jones gave him his pocket book, containing $3. Hill was arrested the same evening. Jones appears like a strong athletic man, while Hill was a small person and weak and puny in appearance. Verdict Guilty. Sentence 5 years in the Reformatory.

James, went into some bushes along the side of the road and cut a stout club from a willow branch. Then they both waited.

A few minutes later, Abel McDonald's wagon came by, heading south. James and his uncle were some distance apart at this time and in the darkness James was unable to see very clearly. But he did see the wagon pass. According to John, James was supposed to stop the wagon and hold the horses, but he either lost his nerve or wasn't quick enough to catch them. The wagon passed on. Ten or 15 minutes later, James heard footsteps heading north. It was his uncle, who told him they had to hurry back to the village as quickly as possible. By 8:30 they were sitting in Mrs. Hill's house with the Barber girls, looking at pictures. Around 9, they went out for a walk. Shortly before 11, the Barber girls went back to Mrs. Hills and the Youngs returned to their hotel, where they went straight to bed.

Abel McDonald was found a short time later with his skull badly fractured. Dr. Hillyear was sent for, but the young farmer died of his injury around 1:30 Sunday morning.

The news of McDonald's murder quickly spread through the town. About 8 a.m. as James was cleaning his boots, the hotel owner told him about it. James asked if the victim was the man who had dined with John the night before. Yes, Murphy told him, then commented that the murderer "would likely be found out." James readily agreed. "That would like be the case, as all such things are generally traced up."[5] Two hours later, John and James Young left Caledonia. They returned the horse to McGee's hotel in Ryckman's Corners. While John continued on into Hamilton, James lingered at the hotel for a little longer. Then he stopped by his sister's house for some fresh clothing before going off to Jacob Young's house, which was closer to where he worked.

James fell asleep on the couch in the front room. When he awoke the next morning, a detective was standing over him, telling him he was a wanted man. James asked what he was wanted for. At first Detective Rosseaux bluffed, saying that he had been fighting with his uncle "Jack" , who was already in custody. But James kept asking, and the detective admitted that he was being arrested on suspicion of killing Abel McDonald.

News of their arrest spread rapidly. According to the *Hamilton Evening Times*:

> large and indignant crowds of people assembled to have a glance at them. Neither of them are prepossessing in appearance: on the contrary, they are from all outward appearance belonging to the rowdy element. They assumed a bravado air ... and seemed to look upon the affair as a huge joke.[6]

After a brief time in the Hamilton jail, the Youngs were transferred to Caledonia, where they appeared before two magistrates. William Sawle, publisher of the *Grand River Sachem,* apparently attended the hearing "Before the magistrates their conduct was much the same as it has been throughout," he wrote. "John indulged in unbecoming merriment, while James William seemed more deeply impressed by the position in which he was placed."[7] The inquiry determined there was enough evidence to hold the duo for trial. John and James Young were sent to the Haldimand County jail to wait for the spring assizes.

Although there was relatively little evidence, the Crown put up a convincing argument and both men were convicted. They were sentenced to hang on June 21, 1876.

Almost immediately, some individuals petitioned for the commutation of the Youngs' death sentences. Their defense attorney, a Mr. Duff, suggested they might have a better chance if they confessed to the murder, which they did.[8] However, John Young was not about to leave his fate in the hands of the government. He began planning an escape from the jail, and he was determined to take James with him.

The two men were confined in separate cells. Conversation between prisoners was not encouraged, and anything they said could have been overheard by other prisoners or jail staff. But John found a way to communicate with his nephew. Using pages ripped from a Bible which he had been given and bits of metal from the bars in his cell window, he wrote notes to James. Then he slipped the notes into the bucket which served as a portable toilet. Each prisoner emptied his bucket in the same place each day. It was a routine task that probably was not watched carefully by the jailer or turnkey who accompanied them, so John hid the notes where James could easily find it. James, in turn, was able to write back to his uncle in the same way.

The system was far from foolproof, however, and the jailer, William Lawrence, found a few of the notes. That should have been enough to put him on the alert, but it was not. On the evening of Sunday, May 28, Lawrence entered James Young's cell to give him his supper. Because James was in leg irons, Lawrence left the cell door unlocked, then went over to John's cell to deliver his meal. After that he returned to James's cell to make up his bed for the night and to close the shutters on the window and lock them

What Lawrence did not know was that both James and John had fashioned skeleton keys. John had used a part from a buckle on his braces and James had adapted a bit of wire he found on a water can. While Lawrence was closing the shutters, James quickly picked the lock on his shackles, grabbed them and hit Lawrence on the side of the head two or three times.[9] He searched for Lawrence's revolver, but could not find it. Then he pulled the keys out of the window lock, where the jailer had left them, and hurried out of his cell.

John's cell was down a short corridor. James hurried there and released his uncle. The two of them made their way downstairs. On the way, they passed the turnkey, who was either sitting or lying on a bed. The man saw them but said nothing.

As they passed through a door at the end of the hall, John turned and bolted it behind him. They left the building by a south door and reached a little gate that overlooked Cayuga. Turning to the west, they ran along beside the fence, jumped it and raced to the edge of the bluff overlooking the river. At this point they were outside the line of vision of anyone coming

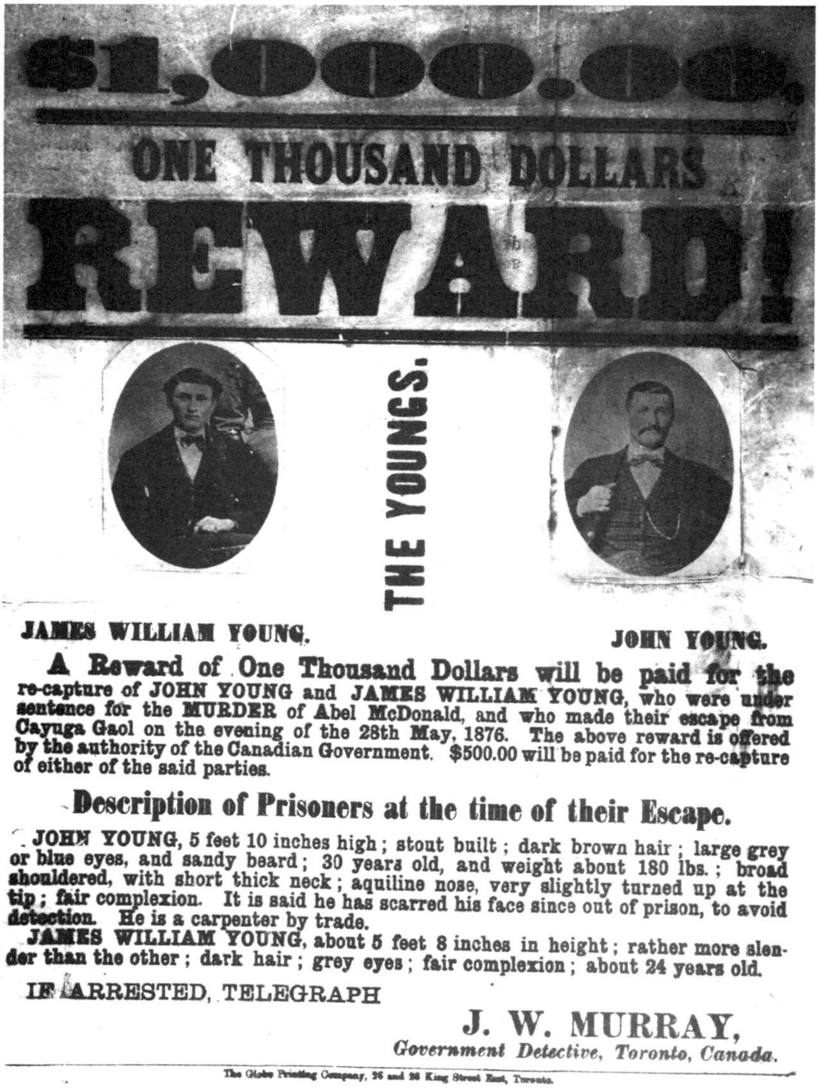
$1,000.00.

ONE THOUSAND DOLLARS

REWARD!

THE YOUNGS.

JAMES WILLIAM YOUNG. **JOHN YOUNG.**

A Reward of One Thousand Dollars will be paid for the re-capture of JOHN YOUNG and JAMES WILLIAM YOUNG, who were under sentence for the MURDER of Abel McDonald, and who made their escape from Cayuga Gaol on the evening of the 28th May, 1876. The above reward is offered by the authority of the Canadian Government. $500.00 will be paid for the re-capture of either of the said parties.

Description of Prisoners at the time of their Escape.

JOHN YOUNG, 5 feet 10 inches high; stout built; dark brown hair; large grey or blue eyes, and sandy beard; 30 years old, and weight about 180 lbs.; broad shouldered, with short thick neck; aquiline nose, very slightly turned up at the tip; fair complexion. It is said he has scarred his face since out of prison, to avoid detection. He is a carpenter by trade.

JAMES WILLIAM YOUNG, about 5 feet 8 inches in height; rather more slender than the other; dark hair; grey eyes; fair complexion; about 24 years old.

IF ARRESTED, TELEGRAPH

J. W. MURRAY,
Government Detective, Toronto, Canada.

The Globe Printing Company, 26 and 28 King Street East, Toronto.

1876 poster offering a reward for the recapture of John and James Young.

from the area of the jail or courthouse. The escapees then made their way to the railway bridge, through Agnew Farrell's woods, then across the road [Highway 54]. Then, following railway tracks when necessary, they walked cross-country to Blackheath.

Meanwhile the alarm had been given. A party of searchers was assembled, but by this time the Youngs had at least a 30 minute head start. It was more than enough to allow them to elude the authorities for several weeks.

Because James and John had connections in Ryckman's Corners and Hamilton, the Hamilton police force was drawn into the manhunt. As soon as they received word of the escape, 14 police officers from Hamilton began searching for John and James. Along with county constables, they planned to scour the countryside between Hamilton and the Grand River and visit "every house where the Youngs were intimate".[10] But it was a slow process, complicated by rumors and false leads.

In addition, there was a certain amount of public anger and quite a bit of finger-pointing. On June 14, the *Spectator* announced that "an Indian from the Reserve" had stated that the Youngs were still in the area and would soon be heard from "as chiefs of an organized gang of desperadoes."[11] The *Spectator* also complained, "No effort is being made to find them, and the sheriff of the county appears to be perfectly indifferent as to whether the Youngs are recaptured or not."[12] The *Spectator's* attitude was ultimately echoed by provincial authorities, who felt that the sheriff, Richard Martin, was incompetent. Because of his advanced age, his son, Deputy Sheriff E.S. Martin, actually fulfilled most of the responsibilities. That did not exonerate Martin Senior from his dereliction of duty, in the opinion of the inspector of prisons. Among other things, he had neglected to appoint a turnkey. Haldimand County Council had actually voted money for a turnkey's salary, but the jailer was allowed to collect it instead. The sheriff was also supposed to visit the prisoners regularly, which he did not do. In addition, when the Youngs escaped, he took his time alerting other authorities. Even his method of offering a reward was criticized. "Instead of offering a *distinct sum* as a reward for the recapture of such notorious murderers, he only stated that a *handsome* reward would be given."[13]

According to the *Spectator,* by the second week of June a definite sum had been offered, $500. In addition, the provincial government had posted a reward of $1000. The *Spectator* argued that this was hardly enough to encourage anyone to risk his life in capturing such dangerous men. Something more had to be done—and the *Spectator* had the answer. In the United States, posters bearing the photographs of wanted criminals were widely circulated, and these seemed to work. Why didn't Sheriff Martin follow suit?

> The sheriff of Haldimand has made no such attempts in the case of two of the most important escapes that have ever occurred in this country. The very idea that two escaped murders under the sentence of death should be at large in the country is terrifying to some and incomprehensible to others, and that there should be no obvi[ou]s attempt to capture them shows a very lamentable state of things in our courts of justice.[14]

In fact, efforts *were* being made to capture them. A wanted poster was printed at the *Globe* newspaper in Toronto. Along with information about the reward offered, the poster featured photographs of both men, plus descriptions. Anyone with information about either man was asked to telegraph John Wilson Murray, the provincial government detective. Murray was also keeping a close eye on certain acquaintances of the Youngs, including the Barber girls.

Nevertheless, John and James were still free. When they reached Blackheath shortly after their escape they were exhausted and hungry. Their first nourishment after the jailbreak was some milk taken from a cow that they came across in a farmer's field. After that, they survived with the help of friends, who supplied them with food and other items. Undoubtedly they stole whatever they could as well.

Initially, they kept moving from farm to farm. James mentioned three farms, one owned by a Mr. Spurm, another by Joseph Hannon, and a third owned by a man named Kerns. Then they came to a farm owned by Alex Binkley, on the first concession near the town line between Ancaster and Glanford. It was haying season and one of Binkley's barns was stuffed with hay. Because Binkley's livestock could graze outdoors for weeks to come, the Youngs realized that the barn would probably be undisturbed for some time. So they settled in. They became so comfortable there, in fact, that the Barber girls came out to spend some time with them around July 23.

Emily and Susan may have been followed, or perhaps they had told someone where they were going. Whatever the circumstances, by July 25 the Hamilton police had learned of the Youngs' location. At 1 o'clock that morning, a dozen officers under the command of Chief Logan piled into two carriages and drove out to the Binkley farm. Leaving the vehicles some distance from the barn, they moved in silently, surrounded the building, then waited for the dawn.

Inside the barn, James Young was sleeping in the northwest corner, while John was lying in the southwest. When James woke up at sunrise, he heard whispering and footsteps outside. Looking through a space between the boards he saw two or three men. Moments later, a board was pulled off the barn.

James hurried to his uncle and asked him what to do. Pointing out that the police had rifles, John said, "We had better surrender."[15] But James had no intention of giving up without a fight. Pulling out his Colt revolver, he went to a passageway that led from the barn to the driveway and tried to make a run for it. As he did, he pointed the weapon at the police, who shot at him. James was wounded in the arm, but kept going. Then more boards were pulled off the walls of the passageway and James gave up. He turned his revolvers over to the officers.

Meanwhile, John had also been taken into custody. "It was but the work of a moment to a pry a board off the barn," a newspaper article reported, then continued:

> and through the opening thus made John Young at once appeared, revolver in hand. Quick as a thought, Sergeant McMenemy seized the pistol, and, in another moment, the hand which held it was in the sergeant's iron grip, from which no prisoner ever wrenched himself free. A single jerk served to send the discomfited murderer sprawling on the grass, and once more he found himself a manacled prisoner.[16]

John and James were returned to the Haldimand County Jail. By this time, William Lawrence had been fired. The new jailer, Peter Murphy, treated the prisoners fairly, but extra precautions were taken to ensure there would be no further escapes. Not only were the prisoners manacled, they were also watched over by guards on both floors of the jail.

John continued to keep up a brave front. He was convinced that the death sentence could not be carried out because the date for execution had passed. But the authorities had other ideas. On September 1, uncle and nephew were taken to Toronto by Sheriff Martin. The following day, they appeared at Osgoode Hall. Their defence lawyer, M.C. Cameron, tried to convince the court that the execution should not proceed, but was unsuccessful. John and James Young were again sentenced to death. This time, the execution was set for September 22.

Some efforts were made to get the sentences commuted to life imprisonment. At first, John refused to give in to despair. His argument, constantly repeated, was that he had never intended to kill Abel McDonald, only to knock him out. Meanwhile, James prepared for the worst. Both men were regularly visited by friends as well as by a number of clergymen.

On September 20, Sheriff Martin received a telegram from the Secretary of State, ordering him to proceed with the execution on the morning of Friday, September 22. When he brought the news to the Youngs, John told him that he had expected it. James, however, broke down. He spent the next few hours in emotional turmoil. When a second telegram arrived. Deputy Sheriff E.S. Martin hurried to James's cell to

The escape and recapture of John and James Young attracted widespread attention. This engraving appeared in the Canadian Illustrated News.

tell him that his sentence had been changed to life imprisonment. Emotionally exhausted, James did not seem to understand at first. Then he told Martin that he was glad, and especially happy that his parents would not have to suffer through the execution.

By this time, construction of the gallows had begun in the southwest corner of the jail yard. John's window directly overlooked the yard. Jailer Murphy asked if he would like to be moved to another cell. John refused. He did, however, ask permission to speak to his nephew.

The two talked briefly, calling to each other from their cells. John asked James how he felt. James told him "that he felt better but could not eat."[17] John told his nephew that, after hearing the good news, he would be able to eat. He also told James that he was glad he had been reprieved and that he felt a great deal better after hearing that his nephew would not have to go to the scaffold. James told his uncle how sorry he was that his sentence had not been commuted. He also tried to offer some comfort by advising John to prepare his soul for the "better world"[18] to which he was going.

John took that advice, asking for various ministers to spend time him. According to Cayuga's Anglican minister, R.J. Locke, he was baptized and took communion during his final days. But he was still agitated and at one point considered suicide. When Mr. Fife, a Methodist minister from Cayuga, visited him, John took his Bible. Left alone in his cell, he removed the clasp from the book and sharpened it against the stone wall. However, he either lost his nerve, or, as Rev. Locke later suggested, realized that suicide would be another sin for which he would have to atone.

John spent his last night in the company of two Anglican ministers, Rev. Locke, and Rev. Elliott Grasset of Simcoe. In the morning, he had a hearty breakfast—two slices of toast, pie, cake and some strong tea. Shortly before 7 o'clock, members of the press approached the cell. John had already met most of them and they probably exchanged brief remarks. Soon afterward, a blacksmith arrived to remove the leg irons. At quarter past 7, the hangman entered the cell and tied John's arms behind him. Constable Farrell then escorted John into the corridor. The condemned man walked with"a firm step" but was "evidently laboring under great mental depression which was manifestly depicted in his features."[19] On the way out, he stopped to speak to his nephew one last time. "Be a good boy James, this is pretty hard, ain't it." Then he paused, and added, "God Bless you."[20]

By this time, other officials had joined the grim procession. Sheriff Martin was there, along with his son, the deputy sheriff, jailer Peter Murphy, two justices of the peace, Ed. DeCew and William Mussen, plus four clergymen, Grasset, Locke, Fife, and Rev. Copp, a Detroit minister whom John had particularly requested. Followed by the hangman they slowly moved down the stairs, out of the jail and across the yard to the scaffold.

Executions were no longer as public as they had been twenty years earlier, when George King and William Blowes, members of the notorious Townsend gang, were hanged in front of the Haldimand County Courthouse. Still, a number of spectators had been invited and were now gathered inside the jailyard. Outside was a larger crowd of several hundred people, including many women.

It was a clear, calm September day, with barely a trace of wind. Slowly, John climbed the scaffold. The deputy sheriff read the death warrant. Then John was allowed to speak:

> I hope it will be a warning to you young fellows not to take my tracks. I see a good many around here that I am acquainted with, and I hope it will be a warning to them and to the strangers too. I don't think I am hardly worthy of this thing, but of course as it is I have to put up with it, and I don't blame any one. What I did do I did'nt [*sic*] intend to do. I hope and trust I will meet you all some day in a better world. I hope you will take warning, gentlemen, one and all, and not come to a place like this. I think this is enough to give you a good warning.[21]

By this time, his arms had been untied. He shook hands with the sheriff, deputy sheriff, the jailer, the hangman, then reluctantly knelt on the trap door of the scaffold. At 7:25, the rope was placed around his neck and carefully adjusted. His face was covered with a hood. Rev. Copp prayed briefly, then Rev. Mr. Locke read the Lord's Prayer, which John repeated with him. Although he was trembling, his voice was clear enough to be heard by the spectators below.

The deputy sheriff gave the signal. The hangman pulled the lever—and nothing happened. Although the trap door had been tested, both the previous day and shortly before John was led from his cell, a link connecting the lever to the bolt supporting the trap door had broken. As John knelt on the trap door, shaking visibly, there was some quick scrambling for a solution. Then someone produced a hammer, the hangman hit the lever and John dropped. He died instantly of a broken neck.

Moments later, the widow of Abel McDonald and her daughter arrived. They had hoped to witness the execution but arrived too late. Instead, they viewed John's body as it dangled from the rope.

After John's body was cut down, Dr. Baxter, the jail surgeon, officially pronounced him dead. In keeping with standard procedures, an inquest was held before a coroner's jury with justice of the peace J. DeCew presiding. The official finding was that John Young had died of a broken neck.

Although friends had asked permission to bury his body, the attorney-general refused their request. John Young was laid to rest in the jail yard, directly under the spot where the scaffold had stood.

Chapter Four

Early Days at the County Jail

The dramatic escape and recapture of John and James Young focused attention on the Haldimand County Jail. Although there was plenty of criticism directed at both the staff and the physical condition of the building, Haldimand's jail was really not any worse than most county jails of the time.

In the early years of settlement in Upper Canada, jails were relatively rare. Legal punishment took various forms, including public whipping or confining offenders in stocks. Fines might be levied in some instances. For more serious offences, especially those involving political matters, banishment could result. Long terms of imprisonment were unusual, as were executions. Up until 1859, capital punishment could be imposed for some 230 offences, including theft, but in practice this was seldom done. By 1865, the number of capital offenses had been reduced to three: murder, rape and treason. Again, the ultimate penalty of law was rarely carried out. For example, when Isaac Lotterage of Haldimand County was convicted of rape on August 4, 1856, he was sentenced to life imprisonment.

Under the district system, serious law-breakers served their terms in district jails, either in Niagara [Niagara-on-the-Lake], Simcoe or London. Once Haldimand County became a separate political entity and the county jail was completed, offenders were usually sent there. For more serious crimes, punishment was usually a term in Kingston Penitentiary, which had opened in 1835.

There were dramatic differences between county jails and the penitentiary. In many instances, those serving time at the county jail were not branded by the rest of the community as criminals or serious offenders. They were ordinary folk, often working-class people with minimal financial resources, who had run into trouble with the law. For much of the Victorian period, especially from the 1850s to the 1890s, Canadian society was changing. The middle class, which had only emerged with widespread industrialization, created notions of respectability which it tried to impose on just about everyone. Punctuality, regular work habits, cleanliness, sobriety and orderly behaviour were hallmarks of middle-class respectability. Eventually, many of these characteristics were reflected in law. As a result, large numbers of working people who did not necessarily subscribe to middle-class ideals were convicted of misdemeanours and petty crimes that would have barely raised eyebrows in an earlier period. Although they might be sent to jail for these offences, they were still valued members of their community. And, in fact, they were often treated as such by the jail staff, who might be personally acquainted with the prisoners or their families.

In addition, many of the inmates in county jails were not criminals. In most Ontario counties, jails were often the only public institutions which could safely accommodate individuals whose behaviour or circumstances made it problematic for them to live in the community. Consequently, aside from people awaiting trial and those convicted of minor crimes, the jails also sheltered the mentally challenged, the mentally ill, the aged and the very poor.

For much of the 19th century, there was no clear distinction between the mentally challenged and mentally ill. Although they were variously described as idiots, imbeciles or lunatics, little effort was made to probe deeper into their difficulties. Those labeled idiots or imbeciles could include people with hearing or speech problems, learning disabilities, autism, Down's syndrome or other ailments. Lunatics might include anyone from schizophrenics and manic-depressives to psychopaths or those suffering from Alzheimer's disease. Some of them might be in and out of jail several times. On

November 29, 1856, Robert Summerville was jailed for insanity. Released on January 7 he was back in jail on January 19th. On March 25 he was moved to the provincial asylum.

When John Woodburn Langmuir, the inspector of prisons, visited Haldimand County Jail in August 1872, he found two prisoners in residence. One of them "had been committed as a lunatic" but at the time of Langmuir's visit "had so far recovered that his transfer to an Asylum as not considered necessary."[1] When possible, the mentally ill and the mentally challenged were sent to asylums, but space was often limited at these institutions and it was not unusual for mentally ill individuals to wait several months, sometimes years, in the county jail. In 1874, Langmuir made two visits to Cayuga, one on April 3, the second on August 21. On the first occasion, there were six men and one woman in custody. He reported, "The latter was committed as insane, but was in fact idiotic, and as there was no vacancy in the Idiot Asylum, could not be transferred."[2] On the second visit, four men and two women were in custody. Both of the women were "insane or idiotic" and were later transferred to a lunatic asylum.[3]

Sometimes, the insane were suffering from dementia, Alzheimer's disease or a mental breakdown brought about by poverty or old age. In a close-knit rural community, neighbours often stepped in if family could not, caring for the elderly or infirm for months or years. But few neighbours were sufficiently patient to care for troublesome individuals who wandered, threatened physical violence or were unable to control their bodily functions. In addition, the financial burden of caring for such people was more than some families could bear, even if the county helped with small allowances. As a result, during the first 65 years of the jail's existence, many of its prisoners were innocent of any crime. When the prison inspector visited on July 11, 1895, he found only two male prisoners housed in the jail. "One of these, an old man of seventy years, was serving sixty days for vagrancy, being simply a case of destitution."[4] Fifteen years later, when Haldimand's House of Refuge opened, the very first resident

Haldimand County Jail Officials 1850-1950

County Jailers[1]

William Lawrence	to 1876
Peter Murphy	1876 - 1885
John A. Murphy[2]	1887-1901
Andrew Williamson	1901-1919
Thomas Walsh[3]	1919-1927
James B. Smith	1927 -1946
W.A. Metcalfe	1947

Jail Surgeons

Dr. Jacob Baxter	? - March 1900
Dr. William Arrell	March 1900 - January 1910
Dr. E.T. Snider	January 1910 - March 1921
Dr. A.G. McGhie	March 1921 - August 1922
Dr. G.V. Simpson	August 1922 - October 1925
Dr. A.J. Bromley	October 1925 - 1939
Dr. R.D. Weylie	1939 - June 1944
Dr. F.A. Vokes	June 1944 -

[1]Dates are approximate
[2]Murphy became Crown Attorney in 1903.
[3]Acting Jailer

Sources : *Minutes and Auditor's Report of the County Council of the County of Haldimand for the Year 1950; Province of Ontario Sessional Papers, various years;* and "The Courthouses" by Monica Walsh, transcript, ca. 1937.

was Mary Cooper, who had previously been living in the county jail. As a local newspaper noted at the time, "Her only crime seems to be that she is aged and destitute and apparently friendless."[5]

Money—or the lack of it—often determined who was sent to jail and who was not. Frequently judges gave offenders an option of either paying a fine or serving time. For many of the individuals sentenced there was no real choice. They simply could not afford to pay the fines imposed by the court, so they went to jail. In addition, through much of the nineteenth century, a man who owed money could be sent to debtors prison.[6] A report covering the period from January 1, 1855 to May 6, 1857 showed 13 debtors convicted of 14 offenses in Haldimand. The men owed amounts ranging from just under £3 to £250 and served sentences ranging from two days to one month. The sentence imposed by the court was directly related to the amount owed, but the time the debtors actually spent in jail depended on how quickly they could raise money, perhaps borrowing from friends or family to repay what they owed. William Thomas, who owed John Reed £22 s15, spent an entire month in jail. But Henry Watson, who owed John McIndoe more than £178 was out in three days. In late February and early March 1856, Thomas Caroll, the only repeat offender on the list, served nine days for owing Richard May just under £8. He was back in jail for 19 days in July, this time for owing May a little over £10.

Many of the offences which brought prisoners to the county jail were relatively minor. Among the most common charges were assault, drunkenness and larceny. Conviction on assault charges could bring anything from a fine or three months at hard labour. Drunkenness usually meant a night in jail or a fine, but longer sentences were usually imposed when there were habitual problems. Punishment for larceny often depended on the circumstances, including the value of the property stolen. Usually the sentence was a jail term of one to six months, sometimes at hard labour. In the worst cases, the court would send the offenders to the penitentiary.

An analysis of prisoners confined in the county jail between January 1, 1855 and May 6, 1857 reveals some of the details of crime and punishment in mid-Victorian Haldimand County. Of the 178 charges, 51 were for assault, 43 for larceny, 35 for drunkenness. Seven men were charged with murder. These included Townsend gang members John Blowes, William Bryson and George King. Also charged were John McKenna and James Stack, who were acquitted, James McGarrity, who was transferred to the Wellington County Jail, and Andrew Hannah.

A Caledonia-area farmer, Hannah had stabbed his neighbour Richard Ferguson to death after long-standing dispute. Several years earlier, Ferguson's dog had killed some of Hannah's sheep and Hannah felt he had not been property compensated. He was found guilty and sentenced to hang. The execution was scheduled for May 19, 1857 but before the death sentenced was carried out his sentence was commuted to 14 years at hard labour in the Kingston penitentiary. Among the other offences that brought individuals to the county jail during this period were attempted murder, stabbing, rape, attempted rape, breaking windows, contempt of court, disorderly conduct, forgery, horse-stealing, housebreaking, leaving employment, maiming cattle, obtaining money under false pretences, perjury, receiving stolen goods, selling liquor without a license and stopping railroad cars. Three individuals were also confined because of insanity during this period.

A closer look shows how the court treated individuals once they were convicted. Christopher Allen, charged with drunkenness on June 25, 1855, was out the next day. In March 1856, he was convicted of selling liquor without a license and spent 20 days in jail. Christopher Carroll, jailed June 2, 1855 for drunkenness, spent two days in jail and paid a fine. He was back on May 14, 1856 for six days in jail. Patrick McDonald was charged with breaking windows in June 1856 and served one month in jail. Convicted of drunkenness in January 1857, he was sentenced to 30 days at hard labour

Other men were also charged with breaking windows during this period, and quite likely their vandalism was the culmination of a period of heavy drinking. Erin Johnston, Michael Howart, Thomas Knichelan and Patrick McDonald were all convicted of the offence in 1856. Their punishments ranged from a fine in Knichelan's case, to 15 days' imprisonment for Howart, and one month's imprisonment for both Johnston and McDonald

If someone left his employment before his contract was up, he might find himself in court. John Armstrong, Daniel McArthurs and John Barrett were all charged with this offence.

Armstrong and McArthurs received fines, but Barrett spent 14 days in jail. Horse stealing, which was at one time a hanging offense, usually brought a jail term. George Hartley, the only person convicted of this crime between January 1855 and May 1857, was in jail about six weeks. A more serious offense was stopping railway cars. Perhaps the men involved were engaged in a drunken prank. Possibly they were railway construction workers with a grudge against their employers. Daniel Carroll and Sellen Taylor were sent to jail for stopping railroad cars on April 4, 1855. Taylor was acquitted and released on April 13, but Carroll was convicted and sentenced to three months' hard labour. A few months later, on August 21, another pair, Michael Duniven and Daniel Donohoe, were arrested for the same offense. Both were sentenced to six months' hard labour.

For men like Duniven and Donohoe hard labour usually meant breaking rocks or cutting and splitting wood. For security reasons, these activities usually had to be confined to the jailyard. Although there are hints that exceptions were sometimes made, it was definitely against provincial policy to allow county prisoners to work outside the jail property. However, in 1880 the prison inspector relented a bit. Because the only work available to prisoners was cutting wood, Haldimand's sheriff was informed that it would be permissible for prisoners to work in Courthouse Park, "provided they were only sentenced to periods under two months and for the most trifling offences."[7]

Most inmates were expected to earn their keep in some way. Many nineteenth century reformers believed that crime was a direct result of poor work habits. Some thought that prisons could teach the skills needed to make a living and survive in the outside world This, in turn, would keep them out of trouble. Female inmates sewed, making or repairing bed linens, for instance. They also helped out in the kitchen and the laundry. Both sexes might take on the task of caring for elderly or mentally handicapped prisoners. Male inmates sometimes did more strenuous tasks, chopping wood in the park or breaking stones.[8]

Confinements and Costs

Haldimand County Jail - 1880-1897

Year	Number of Persons Committed	Most confined at one time	Number of recommittals	Total cost of maintaining jail
1880	87	13	28	$1,710.11
1881	48	8	14	$1,579.96
1882	50	14	7	$1,643.84
1883	42	9	10	$1,662.32
1884	68	13	27	$1,912.65
1885	110	18	39	$2,342.89
1886	125	17	35	$2,128.00
1887	67	9	28	$1,865.61
1888	75	9	33	$2,165.07
1889	122	19	50	$2,027.75
1890	184	27	97	$1,816.90
1891	215	30	140	$1,957.18
1892	130	27	62	$1,905.20
1893	57	10	36	$1,922.32
1894	60	15	33	$1,740.19
1895	106	24	58	$1,903.13
1896	120	22	70	$1,790.20
1897	89	21	60	$1,877.12

The jail, which had between 12 and 14 cells in this period, must have been very crowded at times.

Source : *Province of Ontario Sessional Papers, various years.*

Many government officials hoped that jails and prisons might offset operating costs through the prisoners' earnings. J.W. Langmuir was a strong advocate of this. However, through much of the nineteenth and early twentieth centuries, few jails in the province were able to show much income derived from the labour of inmates. Nevertheless, many of them kept trying. As late as 1932, Haldimand County reported $51 earned from "gaol labour".[8]

Keeping costs in line was an ongoing concern with government inspectors. Haldimand County Jail often paid more for food than was thought necessary. Around 1876, the cost for feeding one prisoner for a day was 25 cents, far too high in the opinion of the provincial inspector. By 1878, after following provincial guidelines for prisoners' rations, the cost had dropped to 10 cents. The cost fluctuated from year to year: by 1929, the average cost of feeding one prisoner for one day in the Haldimand County Jail was 52 cents. Again, this was on the high side when compared to Brantford's rate of 33 cents per day and Chatham's, which was 18 cents.

The high cost of feeding Haldimand's prisoners had nothing to do with official extravagance. Haldimand had relatively few prisoners compared to larger centres, where contractors could make a tidy profit by supplying foodstuffs to the local jails. In Haldimand, the profit margin was too narrow to interest contractors. Without the option of buying in bulk, Haldimand County had to pay more to feed its prisoners.

County council made up for the higher price of food by cutting costs elsewhere. As late as 1869, nearly 20 years after the first complaints were made, the heating system was still working poorly. Bad ventilation, bad plumbing and an undependable water supply were also serious concerns. In 1865, the *Haldimand Tribune* reported that county council had authorized the construction of a large cistern "for the purpose of flooding the cess pool and drain, thereby abating a nuisance which has been neglected by previous Councils."[9] By 1868, and intermittently for many years afterwards, the prison inspector complained of the smells from the toilets and the lack of sufficient water to solve the problem. In 1881, the inspector's report noted that the water supply was "precarious, and very frequently insufficient."[10] There was no well to serve the needs of the prisoners or the jail staff. Instead, they relied solely on water stored in cisterns, which would run dry in the absence of sufficient rain.

Since 1861, the provincial inspector had been trying to persuade county council to modernize the jail. When it was first built, the jail had cells on the upper floor. On the ground floor were more cells, along with the jail kitchen. In the

Above: *The stone wall surrounding the jailyard was built to discourage escapes.*
Opposite: *The gates into the jailyard and a back view of the jailer's house.*

basement was the furnace, a storeroom and the jailer's quarters.[11] Ideally, the facility needed segregated cells for men and women, day rooms where the prisoners could congregate and work, plus some arrangements for separating the more dangerous prisoners from those who had committed minor offences. Year after year county councillors rejected the suggestions. However, the escape of John and James Young provided a wake-up call.

In fact, the Youngs were not the first prisoners to escape from Haldimand County Jail. Security had been a problem almost from the beginning. According to the Haldimand County Council minutes of May 5, 1851, Sheriff Richard Martin was already concerned about the lack of security at the jail. August Niesum, who was sent to jail for larceny on July 2, 1856, escaped during the night of September 13. That should have convinced the jailer to take precautions, but two weeks later, on October 1, Richard Brown escaped. Apparently some measures were taken to improve security, but after inspecting the jail in December 1864, the grand jury reported some serious problems.

> The fence around the jail-yard is in a very inefficient state, and must cause a great deal of anxiety and uneasiness to those having charge of the premises, and we would recommend that the fence be put in a proper state for the better security of the prisoners; and the jury further present that those beaudetts now in the jail be removed, as they can be taken apart and used in the hands of the prisoners as very efficient offensive weapons against their keepers. We would therefore recommend that plank be substituted, similar to those used in the Provincial Penitentiary.[12]

The members of the jury—foreman Samuel Jessop, W.H. Neff, W.C. Lowe, Martin Buck, J.G. Montgomery, W.N. Moote, William McFarlane, William Blackman, William Lyndsay, Abraham Hoover, Samuel Moore, Henry Marshall, William Morrow, Henry Calvert, William Kellam, Samuel Heard, William Bethune, A. McFarlane, Hiram Gee and Thomas Gowland— had done their best.[13] But three months later, recommendations from another grand jury made it clear that county council was not paying attention.

James Thompson was foreman of a jury which also included Robert Armour, Roy Cutler, Valentine Dohn, James Ferguson, Gerald E. Fitzgerald, Isaac Geddes, Ambrose Gloyd, Arthur W. Wright, Frederick McMahon, Thomas Garland. Samuel W. Hornibrook, Robert Kitt, John Lathwell, Caleb Mains, Timothy McMonagle, James Stack, Abraham Wardell, H.J. Johnson and L.J. Weatherby. In their report, the jury members noted "that the fence around the yard is in a very inefficient state, and unsafe for the purpose of properly securing the prisioners [sic] therein confined.[14] The report was printed in the *Haldimand Tribune* on March 2. A few days later, another jailbreak occurred.

This time, two prisoners were involved. One was back in custody by May. A letter to a local newspaper claimed the jailer dealt with him severely. He was confined to the condemned cell, which measured about three by 12 feet and was considered to be escape-proof. "But not satisfied with that, the Jailor, whether to wreak his own venge[a]nce for having to pay the money, or on the authority of some one else, has chained the prisoner down to the floor, and is feeding him on bread and water." The letter-writer, who said the unnamed prisoner had been jailed for a minor offence, wanted an inquiry.[15]

Following the 1865 incident, county council spent some money to repair and strengthen the more vulnerable spots. Four years later, the government inspector described the padlocks on jail doors as "useless."[16] Apparently, the turnkey was equally useless. After another prisoner escaped on the night of October 21, 1871, the provincial inspector investigated and "found that it was attributable to carelessness and neglect of duty on the part of the turnkey, who was discharged."[17]

Five years later, the Youngs made headlines in their daring bid for freedom. In the report he filed following their escape, the provincial inspector detailed some of the problems with the Haldimand County Jail:

> The Gaol is situated on the east bank of the Grand River. The buildings are of cut stone. The Gaol is in rear extension of the Court House, with lean-to additions on north and south ends, giving easy access to any who choose to climb up. To the very windows of the cells. The interior upper flat of the Gaol building is used for the confinement of prisoners. The cells are very badly arranged. There are no day rooms. There is no provision for proper ventilation. The whole interior needs alteration.

Photograph of the jailer's house, 2004. Until the house was completed in 1877, the jailer and his family lived in the jail.

> One yard is used both for airing and working purposes. It is surrounded by a board fence that offers very slight obstacle to escape, being only eight feet high. There is a rookery of small sheds on the S.W. angle that affords additional facilities for scaling the fence.[18]

The Youngs had not climbed out of second story cells or scaled the wooden fence, but the report suggested it was only a matter of time before other prisoners did. The negative publicity resulting from the Youngs' escape finally persuaded Haldimand County Council to make changes to the courthouse and jail complex. While interior renovations were carried out, prisoners were housed in the Norfolk County Jail. Separate wards, one for men, another for women, were arranged upstairs. Downstairs was another group of cells. The kitchen was moved to the basement, which still housed the laundry. Living quarters for staff remained, but this was now occupied by the turnkey.[19] A new house, in the Italianate villa style, was constructed for the jailer and his family.

When the prison inspector made his visits in 1878, he was pleased with the changes that had been made and confirmed that Haldimand would receive a $6000 grant from the government. But county council was still pinching pennies, and Langmuir had to repeatedly request that they install iron bedsteads in the jail. Apparently the prisoners beds were being made up on the floor each night "to the injury of the bedding."[20]

As for the new stone wall, it provided more security than the wooden fence ever could. Nevertheless, some prisoners were prepared to challenge it. Around mid-August 1889, George Browne "made a bold attempt to escape gaol by digging a hole through the wall of his cell which abuts upon the outer wall." Browne was quite a crafty character. Jailer Murphy had temporarily moved him to the women's section in order to conduct a thorough search of Browne's cell. While there Browne found a pair of scissors. "With these he dug a hole about two feet square, half way through the wall, when he was discovered and at once removed to another cell."[21]

Over the next 70 years other prisoners also tried to escape. In 1927, one succeeded, but was quickly recaptured. For the most part, however, the Haldimand County Jail served its purpose of keeping offenders separated from the rest of the community.

Chapter Five

Sex and Scandal

When John Young confessed to the murder of Abel McDonald, he blamed his lawless behaviour on his bad habits, including that of keeping company with the wrong kind of women. Although he made an attempt to exclude the Barber sisters from that group, newspaper readers of the day probably assumed Emily and Susan Ann were far from respectable. Reports that they had spent time with John and James Young alone in Binkley's barn only confirmed that assessment.

According to one source, Susan Ann Barber later gave birth to a child fathered by one of the Youngs, probably James. Although the baby died in infancy, Susan found herself ostracized by the community and died in poverty near Caledonia in 1878.[1] Whether that story was true or not, it reflected Victorian attitudes towards women and sexuality.

Middle-class Victorian women were expected to obey their husbands, look after their homes and families and refrain from any sexual activity outside of marriage. A woman suspected of immorality would find herself shunned by family and friends. This was one of the reasons breach of promise and seduction lawsuits were so common. In 1885, for instance, Mary Featherstone of Rainham Township sued W.D. Ford of Walpole for breach of promise. According to the newspaper report, "after paying her marked attention for about two years", Ford "promised in December, 1883, to marry her."[2] Although a reasonable time had elapsed, he refused to marry her. The jury ruled in Mary's favour and ordered Ford to pay $500.

Underlying the jury's decision were two ideas. First, by monopolizing Mary's attention for more than three years, Ford had kept her out of the marriage market. This reduced her chances of making a match that would allow her to assume a woman's "proper" role as a wife and mother, as well as provide a measure of economic security. In addition, it was understood that an engaged woman might allow her fiancé to take certain liberties that would otherwise be considered inappropriate. Those liberties might not have included sexual intercourse, but extended kissing or fondling would have been enough to reduce Mary's value in the marriage market. In other words, she was "damaged goods" and Ford would have to compensate her for the damages.

Seduction cases were similar, but usually it was a woman's father who filed suit. At the spring assizes of 1885, Thomas Fitzgerald of Rainham sued Joseph Steele of Walpole for seducing his daughter in January 1884. Miss Fitzgerald's name was not given, but her father won the case and was awarded $700 in damages. The newspaper does not provide any details, but in all likelihood Miss Fitzgerald had become pregnant, as this was usually what influenced the court to order large awards. The money was meant to compensate Thomas Fitzgerald for the burden of caring for a daughter whose chances of marriage had been seriously reduced.

At least Miss Fitzgerald had a father who was willing and able to take some action. Maria Colville was not so fortunate. In her case, pregnancy led to tragedy.

Maria was an attractive and shapely 19-year-old. Born out of wedlock, she had sometimes used the surnames of her mother's first husband, Shilder, and then that of her second, Daniel Buck. Maria worked as a domestic servant on several Haldimand farms and in December 1884 was working for Silas Heaslip. Around that time, she paid a visit to her mother in Caledonia and said she was going to visit James Gibson of Oneida. Some time later, when Mrs. Buck ran into Gibson, he told her that Maria had never stopped by. The girl's mother was unperturbed, because Maria had also talked of visiting relatives in Teeterville, northwest of Simcoe, which was a long distance from Caledonia.

Apparently neither Maria nor the rest of her family were much given to writing letters. The weeks passed with Mrs. Buck assuming Maria was safe in Norfolk County. Then she ran into one of her sons, who had actually visited family members in Teeterville. He reported that Maria had never gone there.

Months passed without a word from Maria. In June 1885 William Collver was working on his father's Townsend Township farm along with a hired man, Albert Wisson. While cutting cedar posts out of a swamp, they became aware of a terrible odour. Upon investigation, they found the body of a young woman.

A coroner's jury was held and it was suspected that a murder had been committed. The badly decomposed body was buried in the cemetery beside Bloomsburg Baptist Church. Meanwhile, a detailed description was circulated:

> The deceased was apparently about 25 years of age, height 5 feet 5 or 6 inches, dark brown or black hair, medium length, was evidently a well developed woman; sound set of teeth, all present except one molar in the lower jaw on the left side; was dressed in black or dark green brocaded luster; skirts of checked flannel, white, black and red, red or cardinal stockings; buttoned boots and rubber overshoes; heavy cloth jacket trimmed with satin, yellow and brown woollen knit shawl; ma[g]enta knit scarf and cap made of the same material as dress, in which there was a large pin or brooch; red woolen mitts; lace collar, fastened with large brooch set with a ruby or imitation; plain gold ring on third finger of right hand; pocket in dress contained strong leather purse.[2]

The description appeared in a number of papers, including the *Toronto Globe*. Maria's mother saw it, and after examining the clothing personally, confirmed that the items had indeed belonged to her daughter.

Means and motive were unclear because of the advanced decomposition of the body. However, a piece of cloth around

The Oldest Profession

Until Victorian reformers launched a forceful campaign against it, prostitution was tolerated to some extent. In an age before reliable birth control some people felt it was acceptable for a married man to visit a prostitute rather than risk impregnating his wife, especially if they already had several children or her health was delicate. Similarly, if lusty young men unleashed their passions in a house of ill-repute, there was less likelihood that they would seduce or sexually assault respectable young women.

On the other hand, as clergymen frequently reminded their parishioners, adultery and fornication were serious sins. There was also the risk of acquiring sexually transmitted diseases such as syphilis, for which there was no reliable cure. Finally, there was the exploitation of the prostitutes themselves. They were often abused by their employers or harassed by police, who demanded cash or sexual favours in exchange for ignoring the women's illegal activities.

Because prostitution was tolerated to some degree, the number of cases which actually came to court were relatively few, and in some cases women were charged with lesser crimes, such as drunkenness, disorderly conduct, obscene language or selling liquor without a license. Still, there is evidence that the so-called oldest profession was practiced in Haldimand County. For instance, on September 30, 1868 Susan Wills was charged with keeping a bawdy house, probably in Dunnville. Henry Briggs and William Brooks were arrested at the same time, for being found there. Elizabeth was fined $50 but was sent to jail for 20 days. when she could not pay. Briggs paid his $4 fine to the Dunnville treasurer, but Brooks could not afford the $2 fine imposed by the court Rather than serve 14 days in jail, he ran away.

Maria's neck may have been a handkerchief, and it may be been tied tightly enough to strangle her. In addition, the coroner reported that Maria had been five months pregnant.

At first, there were no clues about her final days. In time, however, bits of information came forward. Instead of visiting relatives, Maria had lived in a "disorderly house" on Concession 12, Walsingham. The establishment was run by Corydon "Cardinal" Smith, a 35-year-old with an unsavoury reputation. Ellen Proper, one of the prostitutes in the house, said Maria went by the name Lizzie Buck and had arrived in late December 1884. Obviously pregnant, she had been in the house about a week, along with other women and Smith's wife. Ellen told authorities that on the last morning of Maria's stay, Smith had gone to Langton for medicine, which he gave to the girl on his return. That evening, he peremptorily ordered all of the women to bed early.

The next morning, about dawn, he was seen driving into the yard alone. A heavy snow had fallen and his horse seemed exhausted, but Smith would not reveal his whereabouts. He did, however report that Maria was gone, and told the women not to mention her name. A week later, the household moved.

Cardinal Smith denied everything. However, the persistence of one man, Lemuel Kitchen, eventually resulted in his arrest. Kitchen theorized that the medicine Ellen Proper described had been administered in hopes of inducing a miscarriage. Instead, Maria had died and Smith hid her body in the swamp. Eventually Smith was arrested and sent to trial in Simcoe in October 1885. However the trial was postponed until the spring assizes. By that time, some of the key witnessed has disappeared. Charles Wesley Colter, Crown attorney for Haldimand County, acted as prosecutor, but had to announce that he had no evidence to offer. The charges against Smith were dropped. The murder of Maria Colville, if indeed it was murder, remains unsolved.

* * * * *

Eighteen years after Maria's body was found, another unwed mother from Haldimand was involved in a crime. Around six a.m. on the morning of Saturday, October 10, 1903, a four-month-old baby was found on the property of Edward Martin, a Hamilton lawyer. One of Martin's servants, Maggie Hopkins, had heard a cry, gone out to investigate, and found the infant near the fence.

The baby (its sex was never specified) was dressed in blue merino and wearing a cape, bonnet and a new pair of shoes. The police were immediately notified and the child was taken to the Home of the Friendless while the investigation began.

Various clues led police detective Miller to the Nanticoke area and a young woman who gave her name as Maude Smith. She admitted to being the mother of the baby. When Maude was arrested, both her uncle, hotelkeeper John Waddell of Port Dover, and Dr. Jolley, their family physician, offered to accompany her to Hamilton. Jolley also went with Maude to the police station. There, realizing that the doctor had been seen with Maude around the time the baby was deserted, police inspector McMahon ordered his arrest.

Apparently Maude had made a vague reference to Jolley's involvement at the time of her arrest. When the pair was brought to police court, Maude was kept waiting in an anteroom while the doctor was placed in the prisoners' pen.

According to newspaper reports, he was a sorry sight, "with gray hair, rather long, and a worn, thin face."[4] Jolley was fiftyish and had practised in Port Dover years. But his practice had dropped off, apparently because of problems with alcohol and drugs. The *Spectator* noted, "He was addicted to the use of stimulants, and took one before leaving the jail...for court."[5]

As Jolley waited for the magistrate to arrive, he stooped suddenly, momentarily disappearing from view. Observers assumed he was trying to hide himself, and he did appear to be very agitated, moving restlessly in his seat. But moments later, he "suddenly stretched back in his seat...his face grew white, the eyes rolled back, and his hands twitched."[6]

It took a moment for the police to realize what was happening. A Sergeant McKenzie rushed into the pen to tend to Jolley, but the doctor seemed to have recovered, and in fact "looked calmly about"[7] telling everyone he was all right. Moments later he "was seized with convulsions. After a struggle lasting about a minute, he suddenly became stiff, and it occurred to those present that he was dead."[8]

Someone chafed his wrists and fanned his face, to no avail. His body was carried into the anteroom, where two doctors were called. They found Jolley was still alive, but declared that he had taken strychnine. He was taken by ambulance to the city hospital, where everyone assumed he would die.

Jolley did not die. By the next morning, the *Spectator* was reporting he would stand trial Saturday. As it turned out, he wasn't quite well enough to face the police court on that date. Instead, his trial was scheduled for Tuesday, October 20.

Long before the police magistrate arrived at 9:30, Dr. Jolley was escorted to the prisoners' pen. Pale and sweating so badly that he kept a handkerchief in one hand to wipe his face, he leaned against the wall of the enclosure. His married daughter hovered over him solicitously, entering the area set aside for prisoners without hesitation from time to time.

Jolley's lawyer, S.D. Biggar, entered a plea of not guilty. He also waived the right to a preliminary hearing. Possibly this decision resulted from Jolley's precarious health. Even as the trial got underway, Jolley slipped into unconsciousness. As Doctors Langrill and McNicholl treated him, he went into convulsions. Once more an ambulance was called and Jolley was taken to the hospital.

While Jolley was unconscious, Maude Smith entered the room and, probably acting on instructions from the police, attempted to enter the prisoners' pen. "Take that girl out of here,"[9] commanded the chief of police. Maude was directed to sit in the area reserved for witnesses.

"A pretty woman, small of stature and with brown hair,"[10] she burst into tears on the stand. Between sobs she answered the questions put to her by the Crown attorney, but frequently her answers were unintelligible to anyone but those closest to the witness stand.

One startling piece of information was the revelation that her name was not Maude Smith, but Christie Van Noon. Before the day's proceedings were over, the charges against her had been dropped. She was released on her own recognizance, on the condition that she return to testify at Jolley's trial.

As for Jolley, he recovered sufficiently to be discharged from the hospital later that morning. He was released on $1000 bail.

On December 1, Dr. Jolley was tried before Judge Snider. Again, he pleaded not guilt to a charge of "exposing a child in such a manner that its life was endangered, or its health likely to be permanently injured".[11] He also waived his right to trial by jury.

Christie Van Noon, who had been married just a few days previously, was the first witness. She explained that the child, whose father was in Winnipeg, had been born in Florida. Because she was determined to keep the baby's birth hidden from her father, when Christie returned to Canada she arranged for a woman in Norwich to care for the infant. When the caregiver was unable to continue, Christie wrote to her aunt Mary Waddell in Port Dover, asking for help in making alternate arrangements, and stating that she could afford $40 to $50 a month to pay for the child's keep.

Mary's husband John spoke to Dr. Jolley, who looked into placing the child in an home in Hamilton. A few days later, Jolley told Wardell he had been unable to make arrangements, but he might have a plan which would be cheaper. On October 8, the physician, Christie, and Christie's aunt and uncle met to discuss the situation. At that point, the doctor told Christie that the Hamilton institution would not take the child because it "did not belong to Wentworth county."[11] There was another way to get the baby into the home, however, one he had tried several times before, and "there would be nothing criminal about it."[13] But he stressed that he would not answer any questions about this method.

On October 9, Christie picked up the baby in Norwich, then travelled to Hamilton. There she went to the Mountainview Hotel, a five-story brick building with an imposing tower on Upper James Street. She presented the proprietor, Joseph Hall, with a letter of introduction from Dr. Jolley, then waited for the arrival of Jolley and her uncle.

The men arrived an hour later. According to Joseph Hall, Jolley was extremely drunk, but went out for about an hour despite his condition. When he returned, Hall asked the doctor and his party to leave the hotel.

Soon afterward, the three of them climbed down the mountain steps, with Christie carrying the baby. At the foot of the mountain, Dr. Jolley took the baby from her and they split up. Waddell booked Christie into the Franklin House hotel, then, an hour or so later, met Dr. Jolley at the Commercial Hotel. At that point, the physician told Waddell that "the child was all right, that he had seen it taken in,"[13] and if Christie wanted to contact the baby, she would have to do so through him.

One of the final witnesses at Jolley's trial was a Mrs. Fuller, matron at the Hamilton Home of the Friendless. Dr. Jolley had contacted her, she said, but at the time the baby was abandoned she had not responded to his request as she was waiting for the board of directors to consider the case.

Detective Miller also testified. He reported that he had overheard Jolley apologize to Waddell for deceiving him. To Miller, Jolley had stated that "he was in bad shape at the time and was not responsible for his actions."[15] He claimed he had not deliberately abandoned the child, but had put it down and then forgotten where he had placed it.

The defense made no attempt to dispute the facts. Instead, they brought in witnesses, including Dr. Kennedy of Port Dover and Dr. Jolley's own daughter, to testify to his physical and mental condition at the time of the crime. According to the daughter, Jolley had been drinking heavily for some time, "and acted very queerly all that week."[16] Dr. O'Reilly, who had examined Jolley after he was arrested, also stated that, given the doctor's condition, he was not responsible for his actions.

Despite Crown attorney John Crerar's attempt, Jolley was found guilty and remanded for sentencing the following day.

The maximum sentence for child abandonment at the time was two years' imprisonment. It was immediately apparent, however, that Jolley would be dealt with leniently. As soon as Judge Snider took his place, the Crown attorney spoke on the matter of suspended sentences. It was his understanding, he said, that a suspended sentence could not be given unless the prosecutor agreed, and he wanted the judge to know that he would agree if that was the decision. To impose a sentence on a professional man like Jolley, he argued, would ruin his life. He also suggested that the judge consider fining Dr. Jolley, or perhaps waiting a couple of months before imposing the sentence.

But Judge Snider had community interests to protect, regardless of circumstances and the concerns of Dr. Jolley's friends. He said as much, then went on to examine circumstances in favour of the doctor—including the fact that he had not acted out of mercenary interests, and that he had made an attempt to place the baby in a home. Nevertheless, the judge "could not overlook the fact that an offense had been committed, nor could he punish some people and allow others to go."[17] Therefore, he would impose a sentence—of one month in the county jail.

Chapter Six
Murder and Matrimony

In July 1857, the *Grand River Sachem* announced "a most horrible and brutal murder."[1] According to the report, on Monday, July 20, John R. Carroll of Cayuga beat his wife to death with a club. Although he claimed that "the Cow had come in the house and killed her,"[2] Carroll was being held at the Haldimand County Jail pending trial.

The next week, the *Sachem* printed a lengthy apology. The editor had rushed the story into print on the basis of information provided by "a leading Magistrate of this County"[3] who had just returned from Cayuga. But the justice of the peace had got the details wrong. There was no doubt that Mary Ann Carroll was dead, but John Carroll would not be going to trial.

The details of the tragedy emerged in a lengthy report on the investigation conducted by Coroner McPherson. The Carrolls lived close to the island in the Grand River. On the evening of July 20, John and Mary Ann were sitting down to dinner with their two young sons. John Pelzner, who had been doing some carpentry work at the house, went into the kitchen and was asked to join them for tea. He refused, but took a dish of radishes offered by Mary Ann. As he reached the gate at the end of the yard, the Carroll's cow approached and he remarked that he wished his own cow would come home at milking time. The cow apparently was let into the yard at this point.

After dinner, Mary Ann handed her infant son to John, then went to milk the cow. A short time later, her older son came out with a cup, which his mother filled. As he was heading back to the house, the cow tossed her head, hitting the boy on the temple. Although the child was not seriously injured, John Carroll commented that he would teach the animal to hurt his son in future.

Mary Ann remarked that the cow was behaving strangely. Possibly the animal was distracted by the presence of her calf, which was penned in the back of the yard. On the other hand, she had only recently returned to the Carrolls' property after spending a few weeks wandering in the bush, and perhaps she was still readjusting.

At any rate, after Mary Ann was finished milking she went into the house with the two boys. John picked up a stick, nearly three-quarters of an inch thick, and started to beat the cow. She ran around the yard, trying to get away, upsetting a number of items.

What happened next is not clear, but at some point the cow went into the house, entering the main room where Mary Ann was holding her sons. Somehow she got out again and in an effort to calm the animal John fed her some hay. Then John went back into the house, where he was shocked to find his wife lying on her back, her head partly against the leg of the table, partly against a wall partition, holding the two boys.

John picked up the two boys, moved his wife to one of the bedrooms, then rushed across the street to Thomas Johnston's store. According to Johnston, Carroll shouted that his wife was either dead or dying and he needed a doctor. While Johnston ran for medical assistance, Carroll turned to Robert Ferguson, a customer in the store, and said, "For the love of God, come over with me."[4] Ferguson followed Carroll back to the house, where he found Mary Ann lying on the floor.

Carroll tried all the typical remedies of the day, loosening his wife's clothing, bathing her face in cool water, chafing her wrists. A short time later, Dr. Jacob Baxter arrived. He also attempted to resuscitate Mary Ann, and at John's request bled her by making a small cut in her left jugular vein. But all his efforts were unsuccessful. Mary Ann Carroll was dead.

Aside from a small bruise on one elbow, there were no apparent signs of violence on her body, but Dr. Baxter ruled that a post-mortem should be conducted. Meanwhile, word spread around the town. The authorities were alerted and a number of questions were asked. Alexander Baird, who was fishing on the point of the island opposite the Carroll house, said he saw John beat the cow with a stick and also saw the cow come out of the front door. The most damning information came from Margaret Lennan, a young woman who worked for the Carrolls' neighbour, John Stewart. Margaret said she had seen Carroll chasing his cow. To her it looked like he was trying to chase it to the door of his house. At one point she lost sight of the animal, but she heard noises as if a fight was going on inside the house. She also said she heard something fall, and came to the conclusion that John and Mary Ann were quarrelling and that he was beating her.

At nine o'clock that evening constable Peter Campbell arrested John Carroll on the street near his home. John seemed surprised, but allowed himself to be taken into custody without a struggle. He also said that he could see no reason for his wife's death.

A coroner's jury empanelled to hear the evidence included Edward U. Sayers, Thornell Hodder, Michael Durkin, Thomas Temple, Joshua Mason, Hugh A. Robb, George Gibson, Mathew Douglass, Samuel Sutor, William Collins, Donald Campbell and Joseph Gibbons, with William Hall as foreman. Although there were rumours that John had beaten his wife to death, no one, not even Margaret Lennan, could recall any quarrels between them in the past or any evidence of physical violence.

Dr. Baxter's medical evidence revealed very little. Except for the mark on Mary Ann's elbow, there was no sign of physical injury or a blow to the head. The autopsy did find "the membranes of the brain very much engorged with blood."[3] No explanation for that was given, but it was suggested that Mary Ann might have died of fright.

After hearing the evidence, the coroner's jury announced its ruling. "We find that the deceased Mary Ann Carroll, was found dead in her own house, and it does not appear from the evidence, that any marks of violence sufficient to cause death were observed; and that how, or by what means, the deceased came to her death does not appear to us the said Jurors."[4]

John Carroll was set free. However a number of people found it hard to believe that Mary Ann had been frightened to death by a cow she milked nearly every day.

Could the cow have been responsible for Mary Ann's death? Was the blood that Dr. Baxter referred to evidence of an aneurism or a hemorrhagic stroke? Or did the physician miss evidence of physical violence? There were too many unanswered questions, and, despite the ruling of the coroner's jury, John Carroll lived under a cloud of suspicion for several years afterward.

Margaret Lennan, the young woman who thought she heard Mary Ann and John Carroll quarrelling may have had an overactive imagination. On the other hand, she may have been interpreting what she heard in light of past experience. In many ways, nineteenth century domestic life was often more violent than today. Although this gradually changed as the century progressed, many people, both male and female, considered it acceptable for a husband to hit or beat his wife if she displeased him. Authorities rarely intervened unless the beatings were unusually severe. Consequently, spousal abuse frequently resulted in serious injuries, and occasionally in death.

On September 23, 1896, Lilly Winkworth Carpenter was found dead in her bed. Lilly, had been married for about a month to Robert Carpenter and they lived on a rented farm at the edge of the Six Nations Indian Reserve, about two miles from Hagersville, a miserable-looking frame building on the road dividing Oneida and Tuscarora Townships. Carpenter was fortyish, a fair-haired, blue-eyed man who wore a full moustache. Lilly was 22 and had been living with relatives. She was a rather frail woman who suffered from epilepsy, a condition that was not well understood and viewed with considerable suspicion in Victorian times.

Lilly and Robert did not get along well. Neighbours frequently heard them quarrelling. On the morning of September 23, around noon, there were angry shouts from the Carpenter household. A few hours later, Carpenter drove to a cousin's home in Hagersville and stayed for some time. When he returned home, he was accompanied by his cousin, Mrs. Giles.

Detective John Wilson Murray

They found Lilly dead in bed. Dr. McDonald was called in. After examining the body, he ruled that Lilly had been dead for some time.

Carpenter immediately started plans for a funeral, but could not obtain a burial permit until the doctor issued a death certificate. Rather than waiting for the certificate, he told the undertaker that he had received verbal permission to proceed with the funeral, Lilly was buried in Springvale cemetery on Saturday, September 26.

When the county registrar discovered this, he informed the coroner. Lilly's body was exhumed in the presence of Dr. McDonald, Dr. Peter Jones of Hagersville and Dr. Howell of Jarvis. Dr. Jones conducted a second examination. He found no indication of disease, but plenty of evidence that Lilly had been severely beaten. There were wounds on her head, extensive elsewhere on her body, and an indentation in the pelvic bone which suggested she had been kicked in the back. On Monday, September 28, Robert Carpenter was arrested.

While Carpenter was awaiting trial at the Brantford assizes, John Wilson Murray, the detective employed by the Ontario government to investigate serious crimes, conducted his investigation. Murray was a Scot who had grown up in the United States, where he got his start in detective work. In 1875, Ontario premier Oliver Mowat invited him to Canada to start the Ontaro Police Force, a forerunner of the Ontario Provincial Police. Murray accepted and spent the rest of his life investigating crimes around the province.

One bit of evidence which came to light during Murray's investigation of the Carpenter was a letter written from a woman in Petrolia to Dr. Jones. They had been married in Waterford around 1888 and had one child, but she had left him because of his brutal behaviour. In fact, she wrote, she still had scars from the beatings.

Robert Carpenter went to trial on December 10, 1896 in Brantford. According to his version of events, he had not touched Lilly. Instead, he claimed she had hurt herself during one of her seizures. If the jurors had relied on looks alone, they might have exonerated him. "Carpenter is not the type of a villain, not a man in whose face murder is written, not a brutal looking fellow," observed a reporter for the *Brantford Expositor*. "On the contrary, he is a fair complexioned and fair haired man, with large bright blue eyes, with a kindly settled smile."[5] But the testimony of several witnesses and medical evidence presented another picture. "If the reputation he enjoys is honestly earned, his looks certainly belie him."[6] The jury found him guilty of manslaughter.

Carpenter took the verdict calmly. "The prisoner smiled the faintest kind of a smile, but a smile unmistakably. He then tugged the ends of his long, blonde moustache somewhat nervously."[7] The following day, he was sentenced to seven years in the Kingston penitentiary.

As soon as sentence was passed, Carpenter tried to say something, but was quickly hustled out of the courtroom and into the jailhouse. On his way to the cell, he seemed "quite elated"[8] over the lightness of his sentence. Then Mr. Wilson, the turnkey at the Brant County Jail, told him that his time might be shorter still if he behaved well. "Didn't I behave well here?"[9] Carpenter asked.

Memoirs of a Great Detective

When John Wilson Murray's book *Memoirs of a Great Detective* was published in 1904, the Carpenter case was one of the stories included. Murray probably recounted the story to a ghostwriter, who sensationalized the details for popular consumption. In Murray's account, Carpenter was a "low-browed, sullen-faced, surly bully", not the pleasant-looking individual described by the Brantford reporter.(Murray also got his name wrong, calling him James.) The detective's investigation led him to the Six Nations Reserve, where, he talked to an "old Indian" he had known for years. After swearing him to secrecy, the elder told him about a ghost, which had been seen running out of a nearby house, utterlng "long, loud, shrill cries".

> ... all in white with its long hair streaming down its back, and its feet bare. It ran through the woods, shrieking as it ran, and waving its arms. The man of the haunted house pursued it, beating it, and knocking it down. It begged for mercy, and would clasp the man's legs, and kiss his hand and his feet like a dog. Then it would fall over, and the spirit would work upon it, making it writhe, and jerking its face all out of shape, trying to turn it into a dog or a cow, or a wild beast. For hours in the, night it would lie out in the woods, and twice it had not even the white robe on it. Then it would creep back into the house after the man who had kicked it, when it fell over, and had left it lying in the woods.

According to the old man, the spirit had not been seen for two weeks. That night, he led Murray by a roundabout route to the Carpenter house. The location, and the description of one of Lilly Carpenter's seizures, convinced Murray he was on the right track. After questioning "the more civilised of the Indians" he eventually put together enough evidence to bring Carpenter to trial.

"Yes, we have no complaint to make,"[10] Wilson replied.

And then Carpenter dropped a bombshell. He and two other prisoners had planned a jailbreak. It was Carpenter's job to knock Wilson out when he came around to lock up the cells for the night. But at the last minute, he lost his nerve and no suitable opportunity presented itself again. "The other two lads were very angry at me for turning them down," Carpenter said, "and I had to lick the two of them at once. I got a black eye in the scrap, and McCosh gashed me on the leg with a knife. I am glad now that I left you alone."[11] So, apparently, was Mr. Wilson.

The Haldimand County Courthouse today. It was completed in 1924, shortly after Nellie Gilbertson was arrested for the murder of her husband.

The Carpenter murder case was not the only one Murray was investigating during his visit to Haldimand County in the fall of 1896. Robert Carpenter's brother Ed was suspected of setting a number of fires on Six Nations land after he had been expelled from the reserve. In addition, there was a curious report from Rainham Centre, where a young carpenter by the name of George Sternaman had died under suspicious circumstances. Prior to his illness, George had been living in Buffalo, and after his death his widow returned there. Murray's investigation led to the exhumation of George's body. When arsenic was found, extradition orders were issued for his widow, Olive Sevenpifer Chipman Sternaman, who was suspected of killing George for insurance money. The sensational trial which ensued made headlines in both Canada and the United States.[12]

One of the puzzles the prosecutors needed to solve in the Sternaman case was whether or not poison had been administered at all. Although a number of scientific tests were available to detect the presence of poison, they were not always reliable. Furthermore, serious digestive upsets were commonplace at a time when wells were frequently contaminated by human or animal waste, meat was stored improperly or food was spoiled by contaminants or poor handling. Stomach cramps, vomiting and diarrhea might simply be the result of eating bad food. But it might be something more sinister, because various poisons were readily available in late nineteenth-century and early twentieth-century households. Arsenic was used to produce green colouring in wallpapers, strychnine might be used to poison rats or other pests. While some attempt was made to control the distribution of these substances, determined individuals could certainly get their hands on them. Frequently, poisoners were women, because they were the ones who usually prepared foods or administered medicine. And, almost as frequently, their victims were their husbands.

In 1902, Helen Nichol, a farmer's daughter from the Hagersville area, married the hired man. George Gilbertson was 29, certainly old enough to make sensible decisions. Nellie, 25, was no prize. She already had a reputation for being "erratic".[13] Nevertheless, the couple wed and eventually produced four children.

It was not a happy union. George's father once commented, "That woman was a regular she-devil. She led the boy a dog's life."[14] He blamed Nellie for his son's failure to prosper, and it seems he was correct. Nellie spent money faster than George could earn it. On more than one occasion she wrote bad checks, and it was not uncommon for bill collectors to show up at the Gilbertsons' house asking to be paid for merchandise Nellie had bought on credit.

Eventually, George was persuaded to commit her to a mental hospital. It was a fateful decision. Although George visited her every Wednesday and Saturday, Nellie was furious with him. However, she hid her feelings well enough to convince him and the doctors that she had recovered. He agreed to her release.

No sooner was she out of the hospital than she started telling neighbours what a “dirty trick” her husband had played on her, and how she wanted to poison him.

In late June 1924, Dr. J.F. McCracken was called to the Gilbertson home at the east end of Hagersville. Shortly after the doctor arrived at 11:45 p.m., George died in agony—but not before making certain statements that aroused the doctor’s suspicions. By the following afternoon, Nellie was in the Haldimand County jail, accused of poisoning her late husband.

Despite rumours that she had suffered a complete physical and mental collapse, a reporter from the *Haldimand Advocate* found no sign of either. Nellie hinted that George, who had been worried about something, had committed suicide. But authorities disagreed. Nellie went to trial in September, accused of killing her husband wit strychnine.

The trial was brief and to the surprise of just about everyone Nellie was acquitted. But she didn’t get of quite scot free. The judge lectured her severely for her vicious tongue and spendthrift habits, telling her she was a “foolish woman” who had “acted unwisely.”[15]

Nellie apparently did not mend her ways. Some time later, she set fire to a house while several children were in it, and, as a result, was sent back to the mental hospital.[16]

Chapter Seven

Mrs. Perkins Goes to Trial

Shortly before Christmas 1906, Henry Perkins boarded a train in Welland. The carpenter was looking forward to spending some time at his home in Canfield and a reunion with Mattie, his wife of 15 years. Near Port Colborne, he ran into a friend, Arthur Hedley, a farmer from North Cayuga. As they exchanged pleasantries, Henry commented that he had never felt better. He invited Arthur to stop by Christmas eve.

Arthur accepted Henry's invitation and went to Canfield on Monday, December 24. He found Henry sick in bed.

Perkins had started to feel ill on Saturday night, but seemed to be better. After a light breakfast, he had walked over to his family farm, which at this point was rented out to Mr. and Mrs. John Darragh. On the way, he suddenly felt very ill.

Mrs. Darragh happened to look out of the house and saw Henry Perkins standing by the barn. At first she could not tell what he was doing. When he came to the house, he explained. He felt terrible and had vomited twice since leaving home. After he vomited again, Mrs. Darragh gave him water, then a mixture of water and salt—a home remedy to help empty his upset stomach. Then she gave him some warm liquor. By this time, John Darragh, who was also feeling sick, had risen from his bed. He noted that Henry seemed to have trouble walking. As he prepared to leave, Darragh told him to wait—their daughter would drive him home.

Henry was at first reluctant, but gave in. The next morning he was still ill, so his wife telegraphed to Dunnville, asking the family doctor to come. When Dr. W. Kerr arrived by train, he found Henry dressed. Although Henry claimed his wife was overreacting, the doctor examined him. Perkins had a slight temperature and seemed a weak. His pulse was slow and there was some tenderness over his stomach, but no other symptoms. Kerr left some medicine and returned to Dunnville. However, when Arthur Hedley arrived at the Perkins home, his friend told him that he did not expect to return to his work in Welland for some time.

Tuesday was Christmas Day but there would be no celebrating in the Perkins household. About 7:30 that morning, Mattie hurried to the home of her neighbours, Mr. and Mrs. John McDonald. Although somewhat older than Mattie, Mrs. McDonald had become a good friend, helping Mattie with the sewing she took in to add to the Perkins family income. Mrs. McDonald promptly went to the Perkins house.

She found Henry lying on his back in bed, very weak and occasionally convulsing. He wanted her to hold his hands. She did so, and he said, "Mrs. McDonald, this will be the end of me." She replied with some encouraging words. "No, Henry, you have had these attacks before and will be all right again."[1] Nevertheless, Henry asked someone to send a telegram to his friend William Spencer, another carpenter with whom he had boarded in Welland. Apparently he sensed the end was near and wanted to see his friend one last time.

Another telegram was also sent, this one to Dr. Kerr, asking him to come as quickly as possible. Dr. Kerr set out soon after he received the message, but missed the train, and was forced to drive his horse and buggy from Dunnville to Canfield.

In the meantime, several visitors stopped by the Perkins place, including Thomas McDonald, Mrs. McDonald's thirtyish son, who ran the family hardware store with his father. Thomas was sent to the local hotel to ask owner Lewis Mehlenbacher for some liquor, which, it was thought, might help Henry. Although Mattie offered him a drink, Henry had difficulty taking it. He seemed to be in considerable pain and suffered repeated convulsions. Then at 10 a.m. he died.

When Dr. Kerr arrived a short time later he was surprised to find Henry dead, but nevertheless filled out a death certificate, citing a ulcerated stomach. However, he explained to Mattie, this was only an educated guess at the cause of death. To be absolutely certain, a post-mortem would have to be conducted. Mattie was horrified and refused to agree. Instead, with the help of family and friends, she made arrangements for Henry's funeral. Jacob Nagel of Cayuga embalmed Henry, who was laid to rest near his parents' graves in the Cayuga cemetery.

Meanwhile, rumors circulating in the small village of Canfield found their way to the ears of Haldimand County authorities. Henry Perkins, it was said, did not die of natural causes. He had been poisoned because, while he was away in Welland, his wife had become involved with their neighbour, Thomas McDonald.

The rumours had been making the rounds for some time. Mattie was extremely attractive. As one description put it, "She is a pretty woman, and altho 35 years does not look more than 26. Pale with large brown eyes, and dark hair prettily coiled on a shapely head, she has the appearance of a clever woman."[2] With Henry working away from home, Mattie was alone for months at a time. While some neighbours would vouch for her "good reputation for industry and morality"[3], others suspected her of infidelity.

Dr. Kerr confirmed that Henry's death had been unexpected and reported Mattie's opposition to a post-mortem. As a result, Henry's body was exhumed and tissue samples sent to the provincial chemist in Toronto for analysis. Dr. William Hodgson Ellis reported that there was enough strychnine in the samples to cause death. A coroner's jury was held in Canfield hall, which was packed to overflowing. Four doctors, including Dr. Kerr, gave their professional opinion that Henry had died of strychnine poisoning. Although there were rumors that he had committed suicide, the evidence was inconclusive. On January 22, 1907, the coroner's jury gave their verdict: "We find that Henry Perkins died by the administration of strychnine poisoning, but by whom we cannot say."[4]

The coroner's jury may not have been willing to say who administered the poison, but there were plenty of others

Thomas Tipton Steele Harrison, one of the magistrates who sent Mattie Perkins to trial for muder.

willing to hazard a guess. Provincial detective Greer investigated the case. By mid-February, the *Dunnville Chronicle* was reporting that he had put together a strong case of circumstantial evidence and that two people would be arrested for the murder of Henry Perkins. In the meantime, Mattie stayed with her father, Isaac Curry, and firmly denied any wrongdoing. "I have nothing to hide," she told a reporter. " I will tell the truth and nothing but the truth. My name has been pure and clean and nothing but what it should be."[5]

On February 19, 1907, having obtained a search warrant, Detective Greer, Crown Attorney John Murphy, High Constable Farrell and Constable Everingham went to the Perkins home. They found a small pill box in a kitchen drawer, which they took away as evidence. In an unlocked desk in the living room they found a book in which Mattie kept records relating to her dressmaking business. Inside the back cover she had written a single word, "ptomaine." The searchers also looked for Henry's trunk, which he had brought back from Welland, but found no trace of it. Asked about its whereabouts, Mattie replied tartly, "It is for you to find it."[6] Although she apparently did not discuss it with investigators, Mattie had already turned over the trunk to her lawyer.

A small amount of residue found in the pillbox turned out to be strychnine. With that piece of evidence, as well as sworn statements from a number of people, investigators felt they had enough to bring Mattie before the courts. On March 7 she appeared before justices of the peace Thomas T.S. Harrison, a Selkirk-area doctor and Thomas E. Cline.

By this time, Mattie had hired a lawyer, Ebenezer Blackie Forsythe Johnston, one of the most famous defence lawyers of the day. Johnston was no stranger to Haldimand County. Ten years earlier, he had defended Olive Sternaman in the same courtroom. Johnston set the tone for his defence when he cross-examined Thomas McDonald, the young hardware merchant suspected of having an affair with Mattie. Under oath, McDonald swore that there had never been anything "improper"[7] between him and Mattie. He had treated her with the same consideration he would have given any other woman.

"Have you ever been pressed to tell a different story than you have here today?" Johnston asked.

"Yes," McDonald replied

"Were you pressed to say that you had improper relations with this woman."

"Yes."[8]

Crown Attorney Murphy objected strenuously to the implication that authorities were trying to railroad Mattie.

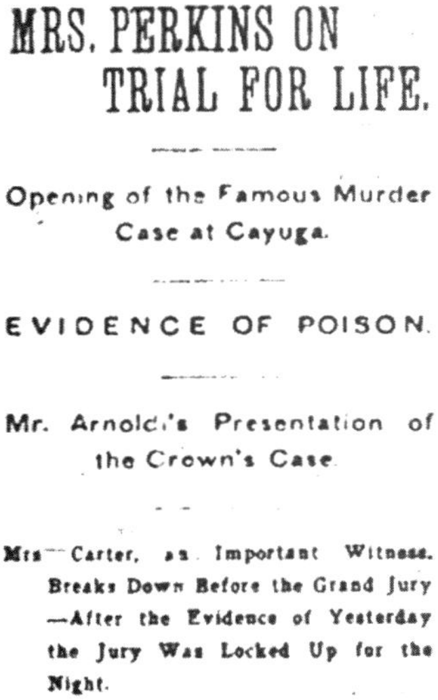
MRS. PERKINS ON TRIAL FOR LIFE.

Opening of the Famous Murder Case at Cayuga.

EVIDENCE OF POISON.

Mr. Arnold's Presentation of the Crown's Case.

Mrs. Carter, an Important Witness, Breaks Down Before the Grand Jury —After the Evidence of Yesterday the Jury Was Locked Up for the Night.

Headlines from The Globe, *Toronto.*

Johnston replied smoothly that he had no quarrel with the Crown attorney, thus suggesting that some of the investigators were at fault. But he reserved his harshest criticism for the magistrates. As the presentation of evidence finished, Murphy asked whether it was necessary to make a closing argument. Dr. Harrison replied that he and Justice Cline had already discussed the case and had decided to sent Mattie to trial.

Johnston jumped to his feet. "There is not a tittle of evidence to show Mrs. Perkins' connection with any poison," he shouted. "I am surprised that in all the county of Haldimand Magistrates would come to a decision before the evidence is all in. I mean what I say and I say what I mean. I am through."[9] Then he pushed his way through the crowd to the door.

Several spectators applauded, but it made little difference. Mattie was taken into custody pending her trial. But Johnston's remarks had apparently hit home. Harrison and Cline felt it necessary to justify their actions and their decision in a letter to local newspapers.[10]

The spring assizes began on Tuesday, April 16, with Chief Justice Mabee of Toronto presiding and J.W. Sheppard serving as acting sheriff. Grand jury members were W.F. Smith of Jarvis; Sidney Best and J.W. McClung of North Cayuga Township; James Duff of Canborough; Valentine Hartwick, of Rainham; Nathan Kelly and James Lindsay of Seneca; William Murray and William Watson of Cayuga; Nathan Overholt of Selkirk; F.J. Ramsey of Dunnville; R.E. Walker of Caledonia and George M. Weiderick of Springvale. Most of the jurors were either farmers or merchants.

Judge Mabee informed the jurors that there would be only one case, that of Mattie Perkins. Before the trial could begin, the jury would have to determine whether there was enough evidence to warrant prosecution. "If you decide there is not sufficient cause to commit her throw the case out, but if you find there is sufficient cause to commit her, it is your duty to bring in a true bill and pass the case on."[11] After hearing the evidence, the jury deliberated for six hours. At 11:30 the next morning they rendered a true bill of murder.

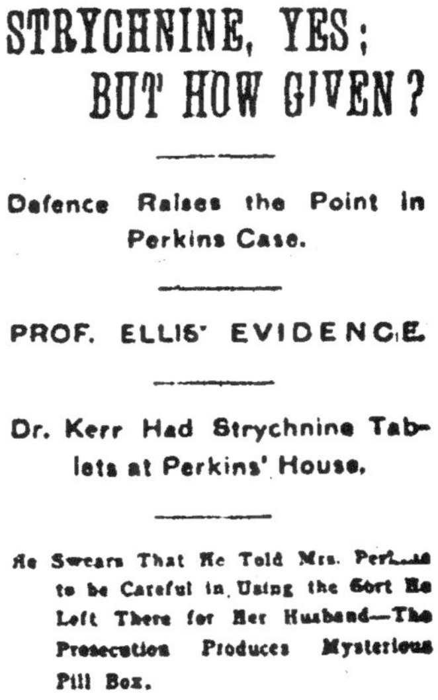
STRYCHNINE, YES; BUT HOW GIVEN?

Defence Raises the Point in Perkins Case.

PROF. ELLIS' EVIDENCE.

Dr. Kerr Had Strychnine Tablets at Perkins' House.

He Swears That He Told Mrs. Perkins to be Careful in Using the Sort He Left There for Her Husband—The Prosecution Produces Mysterious Pill Box.

At one point, Mattie Perkins threatened to sue newspapers reporting on her case.

Mattie was arraigned immediately. She was dressed entirely in black, but had discarded the heavy veil she had worn up to this point. When the clerk asked whether she was guilty or not guilty, she replied in a firm voice, "I am certainly not guilty."[12] Her plea was entered, then, following a request from her lawyer, she was allowed to leave the prisoner's box and sit beside the Gideon Grant, the assistant defence lawyer.

In any criminal trial, the prosecution must establish that the accused had the motive, the means and the opportunity to commit the crime. There was little difficulty in establishing opportunity. Like most women of her time, Mattie handled all the food preparation in the household, so it would have been easy for her to add poison to Henry's meals. Establishing means was a bit more difficult. Several doctors confirmed that Henry had died of strychnine poisoning, but the prosecution had to prove that Mattie had strychnine in her possession.

The sale of strychnine in Canada was carefully controlled, although it was possible to obtain the poison to kill rodents or other pests. In addition, doctors sometimes prescribed strychnine, either in pills or in tonics, because it was thought to stimulate the appetite in patients suffering from various diseases. The pill case that had been confiscated during the search of the Perkins home indicated strychnine had been present there. To link Mattie to the poison, the Crown called on a Mrs. Carter of Walkerville.

According to Mrs. Carter, Mattie, Henry and some friends had visited in the fall of 1906. During their stay, Mattie asked Mrs. Carter for the name of a Detroit drugstore where she could obtain strychnine without a prescription. She wanted to rid her garden of rats, Mattie said. But she did not want Henry to know about the rodents, because it would upset him, so she asked Mrs. Carter to keep their conversation a secret. As far as Mrs. Carter was aware, Mattie had made the trip to Brown's pharmacy in Detroit.

However, strychnine was also a controlled substance in the United States and anyone who bought the poison was asked to sign a book. The Crown's argument centred on a mysterious Mrs. Davis, a Canadian who had purchased strychnine around the time Mattie and Henry were in the Walkerville area. No one was able to locate Mrs. Davis, but it was implied that Mattie had used the name as an alias.

It was a tenuous argument, but might have persuaded the jury if the Crown could present a compelling motive. Some witnesses described Henry and Mattie as a loving, affectionate couple. But a number of witnesses called by the prosecution presented a different picture. Mrs. William Spencer, wife of the carpenter with whom Henry boarded in Welland, told of a visit Mattie had made to her husband in the fall. One morning at breakfast she had commented that she did not want Henry returning to Canfield and lying around the house all winter. Fred Dilse, a railway section-man who had boarded with the McDonalds from November 1905 to February 1906 had seen Mattie in the McDonald house a number of times. On one occasion, he had seen Mattie and Thomas standing by the stove with their arms about one another. He also claimed they were together at a picnic and had been together at a dance sponsored

The Grand Trunk Station at Canfield Junction. Several railway workers testified at the Perkins trial.

by the bachelors of Canfield. Curtis Reece, who worked on the railway water tower at Canfield Junction, once saw Mattie and Thomas arm in arm. Homer Asburn, another railway employee, said he saw them together after they had driven Mattie's sister, Maggie Heaslip, to the train station. James and Charles Burton said they saw the two together in a hammock during a picnic at Lake Erie in the summer of 1906. And Fred Gowling, a neighbour, recounted how he had seen Thomas McDonald enter the Perkins house several times, both during the day and after dark. One night in November 1906, he recalled, Thomas had gone in at 11 p.m. Gowling watched for two hours, but did not see him come out.

Possibly the most damning evidence came from Mrs. Garnett Johnson, a cousin of Thomas who had spent some time in the McDonald household in late 1906. Although she had expressed considerable affection for Mattie in a letter written in March 1907, when she appeared in court she told a different story. She stated that she thought Mattie was "an immoral woman"[13] and that her aunt had deliberately encouraged the relationship between her and Thomas.

Johnston tore apart the testimony about the relationship between Mattie and Thomas. He forced Gowling to admit that he did not like Thomas McDonald because he was dissatisfied with a business deal in which he had been involved. Similarly, Johnston showed that Fred Dilse might have had a grudge against Mattie or the McDonalds. In February 1906, Mattie had told him he would have to find another place to board. After some questioning, he admitted that this was because Mrs. McDonald was sick. As for Mrs. Johnson, she revealed that she had quarreled with her aunt and was no longer on good terms with the family.

As he peppered the Crown witnesses with questions, Johnston got several to admit they had been pressured to make certain statements by investigators. The Burtons claimed they had been persuaded to say that Mattie and Thomas may have been hugging while together in the hammock. Mrs. Carter revealed that, when approached by the Windsor police, she had been asked to downplay a statement Henry Perkins had made. Apparently Henry's father had died after a long and painful illness and Henry had said that he would kill himself rather than suffer through such an ordeal.

A number of defence witnesses also testified that Henry Perkins had experienced occasional bouts of ill health in the past. One Canfield woman, milliner Minnie Moody, told how Mattie had talked to her about Henry's recurring problems, suggesting that if he did not get better he would be dead in a few months.

Johnston did not put Thomas McDonald on the stand, probably for strategic reasons. But he did reveal to the court that Thomas's long nighttime visit to the Perkins house coincided with a time when Mattie was sick and his mother was in the house tending to her. As for the word "ptomaine" which Mattie had written in her dress-making book, she had written it down after hearing about a wedding party that had been stricken with ptomaine in Hamilton during the summer of 1906. She wanted to remember the curious spelling of the word.

Every now and then, a revelation would bring audible gasps from the crowd. There was also a great deal of chattering,

Haldimand County Courthouse some time after 1907. The statue of Boer War hero William Knisley was dedicated on June 22, 1907, shortly after the Perkins trial.

especially among the female spectators. Many of them brought along lunches, unwilling to miss even a minute of the sensational trial. At times, the noise became so loud that the jurors had to ask the judge to impose silence. At one point, when a juror complained, Judge Mabee snapped, "This is not a sewing circle!"[14] He ordered the women to be quiet, then had the constable lock the doors to keep out any additional spectators.

Johnston also undermined the Crown's contention that Mattie had obtained strychnine on her trip to Detroit through the testimony of one witness. Mrs. Clara Buck told the court that Mattie could not have made the trip to Detroit on October 21, the day the elusive Mrs. Davis had made the purchase. From 11 a.m. to 2 p.m. Mattie had been with her at the train station in Windsor.

When it came to the matter of medical evidence, Johnston pointed out other ailments which might have resulted in symptoms similar to those Henry Perkins had exhibited, including kidney problems. He also discussed the use of strychnine in medicine. He was particularly harsh in his questioning of Dr. Kerr, the Perkins family physician. Under cross-examination, Dr. Kerr revealed that he had a number of strychnine tablets in his bag when he examined Henry on Christmas eve. The bag also contained another type of tablet, which Kerr left behind for Henry. Kerr was apparently uncomfortable on the stand, even when answering questions for the prosecution. Often, his responses were inaudible, provoking the judge to growl at the Crown attorney, "If you cannot get your witness to speak out I'll order him out of the box."[15]

Frank Arnoldi, who was acting on behalf of the prosecution, asked Kerr to speak up. Meanwhile, Judge Mabee grumbled, "It is a disgrace to the profession to come here and harass the jury by not letting them hear his answers."[16]

Shortly after 6 p.m. on April 23, the jury retired to discuss the evidence and reach a decision. Around 11 p.m., they returned to the courtroom. Henry Marshall of Dunnville gave the verdict: Mattie Perkins was not guilty.

For a few moments, the courtroom was abuzz. Then Judge Mabee restored order and addressed the jury. "This doubtless is a source of satisfaction to you that you have been able to reach this conclusion. I am unable to say that I disagree with you. There are a complicated set of facts and I am thankful that you were able to arrive at a verdict."[17]

Mattie Perkins was set free. Some of the community believed she had gotten away with murder. Others, noting Dr. Kerr's discomfort on the stand and the testimony about two kinds of pills in his bag, wondered if Henry Perkins had died as the result of a medical mishap. In the end, however, the cause of his death remained a mystery.

Chapter Eight

Justices, Judges and Others

In the early years of Haldimand's history, justices of the peace were responsible for legal matters as well as local administration. Meeting four times annually in Courts of Quarter Sessions, they doled out punishment, collected fines, and in many other ways tried to assure the smooth operation of the area. Some early justices of the peace were extremely influential.

By the 1850s, there had been dramatic changes in the administrative and legal systems in Ontario and justices of the peace lost some of their powers. Nevertheless, they were still deeply involved with the legal system. Typically, justices of the peace — who were also known as magistrates — had little or no legal training. Instead, they were prominent citizens, usually with some influential connections in the community. They could take information regarding crimes, set bail and start the legal process that might eventually bring an accused individual to court.

John Taylor (1836-1902) was a typical nineteenth-century justice of the peace. After emigrating to Canada from England, he settled first in Grimsby, but by 1869 had moved to Dunnville. His main occupation was business: he ran a coal, iron and cement operation and was later involved in the natural gas industry. In 1877 he became a justice of the peace and reputedly "dealt out justice without fear or favour."[1]

As a result of their legal work, justices of the peace were often in close contact with the county sheriff. An appointed official, the sheriff was responsible for summoning jurors for jury duty and keeping records relating to judgements in court cases. He

John Taylor was a justice of the peace and police magistrate in Dunnville.

was also responsible for ensuring that court orders were carried out. It was the sheriff who directed the bailiff to seize property; it was also the sheriff who presided at executions. The sheriff's other duties included appointing jailers and keeping order in the courtroom, usually by assigning constables to ensure discipline was maintained.

Haldimand County's first sheriff was Richard Martin. Born in Connemara, County of Galway, Ireland in 1797, Richard was the son of Richard "Humanity" Martin, the man who successful sponsored introduction of controversial British legislation for prevention of cruelty to animals. In 1833, with his wife Emily Sylvia Kirwan, Richard emigrated to Canada and settled in Seneca Township, near York. Four years later, when the 1837 Rebellion erupted, he served in the militia and was stationed for several months near Chippawa [Niagara Falls]. When he returned to Seneca Township, he raised a volunteer company and eventually became colonel of the Haldimand militia.

Richard Martin, first sheriff of Haldimand County.

Martin was appointed Haldimand County's first sheriff in 1850 and held the position until his death in 1878. However, during much of that time, the actual duties of the office were carried out by one of his sons, Evan Stratford Martin, who was appointed deputy-sheriff in 1851. Three other sons, Richard, Edward and John Robert, practised law. Richard and Edward eventually moved to Hamilton, but John Robert served as the clerk of the peace in Haldimand County and later County crown attorney.

Another Irishman followed Richard Martin as Haldimand's second county sheriff. Robert H. Davis (1828-1907) was born in Eniskillen, Ireland and arrived in Canada around 1850. Like Martin, he also settled in Seneca Township. As a youth in Ireland he had worked with an apothecary and his interest in medicine continued after his arrival in Canada. Shortly after settling in Haldimand he enrolled in medical studies and in 1856 began a practice in York. Like Martin, he was also active in the militia. According to his obituary, Robert Davis was:

> a man of very strong personal feeling, who made attachments which he continued during his lifetime. He was noted for his genial, courteous manner and unbounded charity, and his

Robert H. Davis, second sheriff of Haldimand County.

> disposition could be summed up in the few words, a real Irish gentleman.[2]

He was also noted for his dignified bearing and his promptness — when he was in charge, court usually started on time.

Harrison Arrell, right, *served as county Crown attorney, county clerk and county solicitor. Here he swears in A. Earl Catherwood, a member of Haldimand County Council in the late 1940s.*

County Judges

Like early justices of the peace, early judges did not necessarily have extensive legal training. Bernard Foley, Haldimand's first county judge, was typical of this breed. An affable, humourous man from St. Catharines, Foley was known for his girth and enjoyment of a good time. Like most men of the middle to late nineteenth century, he thoroughly enjoyed alcoholic beverages. Foley, however, seemed to know when to draw the line. One of his successors, M.C. Upper apparently did not. Upper was Haldimand's third county judge. He had settled in Dunnville in 1864, where he practiced law and served as a member of the town's first high school board. Upper was appointed county judge in 1884, but as time passed his consumption of alcohol caused problems. He drank so much that complaints were sent to the provincial justice department and an investigation was launched. During the investigation, county clerk James Mitchell testified that he had not seen the judge drunk while presiding over court for 18 months. Then, the story goes, he pointed out that Upper had not been in court for 18 months!

Eventually, Upper's drinking ended his career as a judge. After receiving a letter stating that more complaints had been sent to Toronto, Upper decided to submit his resignation. When he sobered up, he tried to retrieve the letter, but was too late. His resignation was accepted and Upper was replaced by Judge D. MacMillan.

Compared to Foley and Upper, John Gustavus Stevenson was a prince among judges. Haldimand's second county judge was born in Lincoln County on June 1, 1818. His father was an Irish immigrant, but his mother's father was Robert Addison, one of the pioneer clergymen of Upper Canada and a prominent member of Niagara society. Stevenson was educated at Upper Canada College and from 1840 to 1842 practiced law in the Niagara area. Then he moved to St. Catharines, where he worked as clerk of the United Counties of Lincoln, Welland and Haldimand. In 1851 he moved to Cayuga to take up duties as clerk of the peace and in 1855 was appointed county judge. According to one biographer, Stevenson was "affable and courteous" a "polished gentleman" who was a "sound and thorough" lawyer "and when in practice was one of the foremost advocates in this part of the Province." As a judge, he was "very careful and accurate in making up his judgements ... very impressive and often truly eloquent."[3]

Another highly respected Haldimand county judge was Charles Wesley Colter, (1846 -1929). Born to Irish immigrants in New Brunswick, he graduated from the University of New Brunswick with degrees in English and classics. Colter taught high school in New Brunswick, Cayuga and Dunnville and was the first principal at Dunnville's high school. Around 1872-1873 he published the *Monck Reform-Press*, a Dunnville based newspaper, then spent two years working for Canadian immigration services in England. When he returned to Canada

Robert F. Miller, left, *served as county warden in 1898 and was appointed county sheriff in 1935. He is shown here around 1950 with two other former wardens, J.J. Parsons,* centre *and William G. Clark* right.

in 1876 he enrolled in law school and was called to the Ontario bar in 1879. While practicing in Cayuga he also entered politics and was elected to the Ontario legislature in 1886 and 1889. In 1903, he replaced Judge D. MacMillan as Haldimand county judge. The following year he was made a senior judge and transferred to Elgin County.

Judge Colter divided his time between his home in St. Thomas and a summer home in Port Stanley . When he died at his cottage in 1929, the *Simcoe Reformer* noted that as a politician he had been "one of the ablest and most vigorous campaigners of the day." As a judge, "he enjoyed the reputation of being manifestly fair-minded and never unduly severe in his judgements. ... As a politician, Judge Colter was regarded as being one of the ablest and most vigorous campaigners of his day."[4] Harrison Arrell, who served as Haldimand's county Crown attorney for more than 30 years, called Colter "a man of fine natural ability ... with a good knowledge of the law."[5] If he had one flaw, it was that he was always late for court, sometimes delaying proceedings by an hour or more.[5]

Inauguration of Helen Kinnear as county court judge, 1954. L-R: *county court judges D.J. Cowan (Brant), J.G. Stuart Stanbury (Lincoln) and E.S. Livermore (Norfolk).*

Helen Kinnear

Every county court judge made his own unique contributions to Haldimand County. But one judge brought the area a degree of fame in legal circles. This was Helen Kinnear, the first woman in Canada to be appointed to a county bench.

Helen A. Kinnear was born in Cayuga on May 6, 1894, one of four children of Louis Kinnear and Elizabeth Eleanor Thompson. She received her early education in Port Colborne, where her father practised law. Helen later attended high school in Welland and in 1917 graduated from the University of Toronto with honours in English and history. Then it was on to Osgoode Hall to study law. By the time she was finished her first year, she had won a scholarship.

After graduating with honours in 1920, she joined her father's law firm. At the time, the legal profession was dominated by men. Helen ignored most of the barriers, breaking new ground in the process. She was the first female lawyer to appear before the Supreme Court of Canada, the first woman in Welland County to appear before the Supreme Court of Ontario, and in 1934 she became the first woman in the British Empire to become a King's Counsel.

Judge Helen Kinnear.

Nine years later, she made legal history again when she was appointed county court judge for Haldimand. Her success was supported by a number of other women across the province. When she was sworn in at the Haldimand County Courthouse, members of the Women's Law Association of Ontario travelled to Cayuga to witness the ceremony. Members also honoured her achievement by giving a dinner for her at the Toronto University Women's Club on July 3.

Like many lawyers, Kinnear took an active interest in politics, serving as president of the Welland County Liberal Association for two years, and in 1941 winning the Liberal nomination for the county. But women in politics were still a rarity, and in the best interest of the party she made the difficult decision to step aside to allow Humphrey Mitchell, newly appointed minister of labour, to run in a by-election.

Although a political career was not in the cards for her, Judge Kinnear had plenty to do. She was particularly interested in the plight of children, prisoners and the insane and spent much time serving on the bench of juvenile and family courts. After she moved to Haldimand, she became honorary president of the county's Children's Aid Society. She also served as first president of the Juvenile and Family Court Judges Association of Ontario from 1952 to 1954. On March 2, 1954 she was appointed to a royal commission into criminal law relating to the defence of the insane. Later that month she was appointed to a second royal commission, this one involved in amending the law on criminal sexual psychopaths.

Judge Kinnear was a strong supporter of women's rights. In 1952, as Ontario women were finally being allowed to sit on juries, Kinnear was asked what she thought of the change. At the time she was Canada's only female judge. Her response was blunt. "Why not? I had to pick out the names of men for jury duty for nine years. I got a bit tired of it."[6]

In 1965, two years after she retired and returned to live in Port Colborne, Judge Kinnear became the first woman to receive a medal and citation from the John Howard Society of Ontario. The Society, which is dedicated to assisting prisoners, cited her "distinguished humanitarian service."

Judge Kinnear died in 1970 at the Port Colborne General Hospital. On International Women's Day, March 8, 1993, Canada Post introduced four stamps honouring Canadian women of achievement. Among them was Judge Helen Kinnear.

Chapter Nine
Strange Crimes and An Unusual Punishment

The train station in Jarvis, like every train station in the world, has been the scene of much drama. There have been tearful departures, joyful homecomings, holiday excitement as excursion trains pulled out for Niagara Falls or Toronto's CNE. The Jarvis station has seen it all since the Great Western Airline track went through in 1872.

Two years later, the station house went up. Before it was destroyed in a 1912 fire, the Jarvis train station played a role in one of the most bizarre crimes in Haldimand history.

Shortly before Christmas 1910, the *Jarvis Record* ran a front page story reporting that a body of a man had been found in a barrel in Montreal. The barrel, which was supposed to contain turkeys, had been shipped from Jarvis.

The paper described the man as about 70, with a white hair and beard, and asked, "Does anyone know such a person being missed from this locality?"[1]

By December 28, the newspaper had more details. The man in the barrel was Matthew Johnston, the recently deceased caretaker of Knox Presbyterian Church. His body had been shipped to a medical school affiliated with McGill University. James Johnston, his son, had travelled to Montreal, identified his father's body, and brought it back to Jarvis for reburial.

In the meantime, investigators had arrested John McSorley. An eccentric character who had studied medicine in Montreal and Philadelphia, McSorley was nicknamed Doc, although he had never received his medical license. He was in the habit of carrying lancets in his pocket, pulling them out to show to acquaintances, and talking at great length about his experiences in medical school. "Consequently he was treated with considerable aloofness," noted the *Record*, "especially since he had his head injured several years ago, in a fall from a train, and ever since he had suffered from its effects."[2]

Doc had apparently boasted that medical schools would pay him $25 for every cadaver he delivered. According to evidence presented at his trial, he was seen pushing a wheelbarrow into the cemetery of Knox Church on November 22. Another witness saw him carrying a heavy barrel from a nearby shed, and it was this barrel that was eventually shipped to Montreal. John McSorley was found guilty and sentenced to five years in Kingston Penitentiary.

* * * * *

Today, John McSorley probably would have been confined to a mental institution. But these facilities were not used as frequently in the late 1800s and early 1900s. Furthermore, there was very little difference between prisons and mental hospitals. at this time. This was one of the reasons family members did what they could to keep their loved ones out of mental institutions. While they were probably motivated by the best intentions, allowing a violent, mentally disturbed individual to remain at large could lead to tragedy as it did near Selkirk in 1920.

In the late spring of that year, a Selkirk-area resident, Mrs. Thomas Badley, died. She was survived by her husband, a farmer and expert sheep-shearer, and two grown children, George and Elizabeth.

George was 38. Like many adult children of the era he had gradually taken over the responsibilities of the farm as his parents aged. Elizabeth, who was a few years younger, was another matter. According to the *Haldimand Advocate*, she was "said to have been of unbalanced mind for fifteen years or more and rumors are current that she was quite violent at times."[3] Despite Elizabeth's condition, her mother had cared for her at home, although she often had to lock Elizabeth in her room. On her deathbed, Mrs. Badley made George promise to continue to care for his sister, and he agreed.

The original Jarvis train station burned in 1912.

On May 17, a tombstone salesman from Simcoe called at the Badley farm. Thomas was away on business at the time, and at first George was nowhere to be seen. Like most visitors to rural areas, the salesman knew that if no one opened the door at the house the most likely place to try next was the barn. When he did so, he found George with his throat slashed.

A doctor and Constable Harry Lamb of Selkirk were called to the scene. George's wound was not life-threatening, although it required several stitches to close. But the constable's investigation revealed more horror in the house. Elizabeth's skull had been crushed and her throat was cut. Questioned, George admitted killing his sister. He was arrested and sent to the county jail in Cayuga.

Coroner Dr. Quance of Hagersville ordered an inquest, which was held on May 20 with Magistrate J.E. Hoover presiding. The coroner's jury, which included William Cronk, Harvey Martin, Court Evans, Joseph Steel, Burton Hurst, Arthur Gillies, George Roth, Joseph Cronk and Ellis Bartlett, heard George testify that he had killed his sister with a piece of gas pipe. According to a report in the *Haldimand Advocate*:

> He took the full responsibility for his crime, giving the excuse that i[t] was for his sister's good. He had preserved clippings from some foreign papers where expressions were given that when a person was in the condition in which his sister was, it were better that they be put of the way."[4] He also told the jury that he had promised his mother he would not let his sister be taken away to an asylum, but "she was so vicious at times that it was hell, and conditions were beyond management.[5]

The jury brought in a verdict of wilful murder and George was ordered to stand trial. He was returned to the county jail in Cayuga, where the staff was told to watch him carefully.

On the morning of June 8, two alienist, as psychiatrists were then called, examined George in his cell. Around 2:30, Dr. Snider, who cared for the prisoners, dressed George's wound. Late that afternoon, George was let out of his cell and into the corridor for exercise. Around 5, he was left alone for a few moments. When jailer Walsh and the guard returned, they found he had hanged himself from his cell door with a towel.

Once again, a coroner's jury was summoned. J.E. Fissette, G. H. Fissette, James Harkins, Ray McDonald, Sam Brooks, William Harkins, John Carryer, William Ralston, Peter Doyle and W.H. Kindree listened as Walsh testified that "Badley seemed to be quiet and didn't show any signs of insanity."[6] Murphy, the jail guard, said, "He didn't see anything wrong with him out of the ordinary. He seemed quiet, and would answer when spoken to."[7] But Dr. Snider admitted he "seemed nervous and despondent Tuesday afternoon."[8] Not surprisingly, the coroner's jury ruled that George had committed suicide.

And there the matter ended. Today, there would have been newspaper and magazine articles, interviews and expert analyses of the situation that led to Elizabeth's murder and George's suicide. There probably would have been considerable sympathy for George. But the 1920s were a different time, with different social institutions and different values. Ultimately, George and Elizabeth were both victims of the society in which they lived.

There was no evidence of mental illness in another tragic case a couple of years later. However, it might be argued that the perpetrators were not in full possession of their faculties. In this instance, they were handicapped by their youth.

At various times in history, authorities have taken different approaches to youthful criminals. Sometimes, they were treated like adults and subject to the full penalty of the law, including execution. And murder wasn't the only capital crime—at various times in our history, a child or teenager could have hanged for what we'd now consider petty theft. But there were also periods when legal authorities took a very lenient view of young offenders. Youthful high spirits were frequently cited as the reason behind pranks that destroyed property or injured people. Depending on the damage, young offenders might get off with a warning or a fine.

Sometimes, though, pranks could lead to disaster. In the fall of 1922, a new concrete bridge was under construction on Highway 3, east of Jarvis. To allow traffic to pass over Stoney Creek, a temporary bridge had been erected on the south side of the road, and the old bridge demolished. Barricades were erected across the road to prevent unwary motorists from plunging into the creek.

Car lights were relatively weak compared to those used today, and reflective material was rarely used on road signs. So, to increase visibility, a red warning light was placed in front of the barricade at night.

Sometime after 12:30 a.m. on Sunday, October 29, the light was removed by pranksters. In the early hours of Sunday morning, Dr. John J. Jaques, a 38-year-old Fisherville veterinarian, was returning from a visit to family in Simcoe. With him was his son, Carl. Dr. Jaques had gone to Simcoe by a different route, and was unaware of the construction. So he had no warning when the car struck the barricade and fell 10 feet into the creek.

Carl escaped and tried desperately to free his father. But Dr. Jaques was pinned beneath the steering wheel. Before Carl could bring help, his father drowned.

At the inquest that followed, the coroner ruled that Jaques had met his death through the actions of person or persons unknown. The community was outraged. One newspaper editorial commented:

> The only charge that can be made in case of this description is one of 'murder'....We hope that the guilty party or parties may be apprehended and made to suffer the maximum punishment for their dastardly crime. It matters not whether the warning lights were taken as a joke or was the work of thieves, for the result is the same, and a man who was greatly respected...was rushed into eternity without the slightest warning of his impending fate.[9]

The Ontario Department of Highways offered a $500 reward for information leading to the arrest of the culprits. That, police investigation and public sentiment eventually led to the arrest of five youths.

They were tried for manslaughter in the fall of 1923. All five pled guilty. Before sentencing, however, Judge Lennox gave them three weeks to consider how they might make restitution to the widow. When they returned to the court, each of the five offered to pay Maud Jaques $500. The widow and the court agreed, and the boys were given suspended sentences, placed under a $1,000 peace bond, and ordered to pay $5 a week to the widow over the next two years.

It was an unusual and thoughtful sentence, sound in theory. In practice, it was far from perfect. Although two of the boys fulfilled their promise, the other three did not. One paid just $195, another $55, and the third $20.

Documents in the possession of Carl's son Lynn showed that considerable effort was made to have the payments continue. Lawyers were hired to sue for the money, but to no avail. Eventually, the Jaques family simply stopped trying, and three of the young men responsible for the death of Dr. Jaques went virtually unpunished.[10]

Chapter Ten

Unsolved Murders

During the construction of the Welland Canal and the Feeder Canal linking it to the Grand River, hundreds of workers were brought into eastern Haldimand. Most were Irish immigrants and many of them were accompanied by their families. Although most labourers were willing to work, paying jobs were not always easy to find. Most experienced long periods of unemployment and as a result almost always lived a precarious hand-to-mouth existence. Because their resources were so scarce, they often stole what they needed, including the scrap lumber with which they built the shanties they called home. As they tended to live together on the edges of towns, these makeshift communities were often nicknamed Slabtown. St. Catharines had a Slabtown and so did Dunnville.

Dunnville's Slabtown had started around 1830 or so. By the 1880s, day labourers, railroad workers and descendants of canal workers all congregated here. Almost all of them were squatters who had no real claim to the land on which they lived. To outsiders, Slabtown was an unsavoury area full of violence and a dangerous place to visit after dark. Its residents had their own culture and their own rules. They were "a motley population" according to Ontario provincial detective John Wilson Murray, "who lolled through life with an occasional industrious man among them. ... as distinct, in their way, as a nation apart from Canada, for they seem to have a code of morals all their own. ..."[1] According to Murray, it was not unusual for men to trade wives with alarming regularity, bargaining away their spouses for a dog, a knife, or other items.

On October 31, 1888, a Toronto harnessmaker named Lowrie was in the Dunnville area. He had been drinking heavily before wandering into Slabtown around 5 p.m. that evening. He never returned. Around 11 p.m., John Upper, who lived near the canal, heard a scream, a splash, and the sound of someone running across the bridge. After daylight a number of people investigated and found no traces of an accident or a fight. But Lowrie had vanished, along with the large sum of cash he was carrying with him.

On November 9, his body was found floating in the canal. His skull had been smashed and someone had gone through his pockets. The authorities were alerted and John Wilson Murray came from Toronto to investigate.

Wilson's inquiries led him to Joe Clemo, a "bad egg" who had already served time in the penitentiary and was known as a troublemaker. Clemo was nearly always broke. On October 29, he had borrowed a nickel from someone. But two days later, when he visited Henry Overhold, he told him he would be a rich man before morning.

That night, someone murdered Mr. Lowrie. A short time later, Clemo called on a woman named Huldy Smith. Although Huldy was married to Joe Williams Smith, Clemo tried to convince her to run away with him. Huldy later repeated their conversation to Detective Murray.

"Joey showed me the squidge of bills, and he shook them to me so's I smelt 'em, and he says to me: 'Huldy, fly with me to the United States,'" Huldy recalled.

"Was that all he said?" the detective asked.

"Oh no," Huldy replied. "He says he love me and I smelt the bills again. Bills has a funny smell."

"Didn't Joey tell you where he got the bills?"

"No, I didn't ask."

"But if Joey really had loved you he would have told you where he got them."

Huldy bristled. "Huh! So he did tell me. While I was smelling the bills Joey Clemo whispers to me, 'Huldy I love you; fly with me; and I killed an old man because I had to hit him to rob him, and I hit him harder than I meant, so when he wouldn't come to I pitched him in the canal. Fly with me.'" Then, to make it clear to Murray that she did not condone Clemo's actions, Huldy added, "I told Joey that was no way to get money, and for him to go on about his own business and fly himself, but he wouldn't fly me with him. I stood by for John William, who ain't hitting people too hard on the head and pitching bodies into the canal."[2]

Possibly Huldy was also deterred by Clemo's appearance. According to Murray, he was "the hardest-looking man in the dock I ever saw. He was cross-eyed, so that he seemed to hold his head sidewise to see you."[3]

Clemo apparently did "fly" soon after Lowrie's death. It took Murray several months to track him down, but on April 4th he arrested him in Essex County. He was brought back for a preliminary hearing, where it was decided there was enough evidence to send him to trial.

Meanwhile, according to Murray, various female residents of Slabtown were competing for a bit of local fame by claiming Joe Clemo had also asked them to elope with him.

> When Huldy Smith said Joe had asked her first, another promptly declared Joe Clemo had asked her three times. ... One of the women finally said that Joey embraced her and said: "You need not fly with me, if you don't want to. I love you so that you can take the money and not fly." [4]

In this case, the woman refused the money.

As other witnesses were questioned, it became clear to Murray that they were not as interested in telling the truth as they were in spinning a good yarn. By the time Clemo came to trial, Murray had serious misgivings. As he told Crown Prosecutor Colin Macdougal he was convinced Clemo had killed Lowrie, but he did not think the witnesses were being truthful. He also suggested that Macdougal alert Judge Armour to the situation.

> I knew there would be no restraining many of the witnesses, once they got on the stand. They would simply vie with one

Price' Farmers Hotel, built in 1901, was a favourite haunt of murder victim Lorne Moss.

> another to tell the biggest story and make the grandest appearance on the witness stand. She who carried off the honours would be the queen of Slabtown, and her various children would bask in her glory.[5]

Murray and Macdougal worried about the Crown witnesses' lack of credibility, knowing that in the hands of a competent defense lawyer the case against Joe Clemo would crumble. The testimony of Sarah Scollie, *aka* Sally Poney, was typical. Sarah had been living with Sam Smith, a crony of Joe Clemo. Murray suspected Smith had played a part in Lowrie's death, but there was insufficient evidence to bring him to trial.

Clemo's lawyer, Mr. Snyder, started off with a seemingly innocuous question. "Are you married, Sarah?"

"None of your — business," she replied disdainfully. The judge ordered her to answer the question."Not by a — sight," she snapped.

Snyder then asked who she was living with.

"Sam Smith."

"How long have you lived with Sam?" Snyder asked.

"Two years."

"With whom did you live before that?"

"Ben Hughes." By this time, Sarah was growing angry.

"How long?"

"About a year and a half."

"Was there not a dicker between Sam Smith and Ben Hughes about your transfer?"

Tossing her head and giving Snyder a look of "unutterable scorn," Sarah snapped, "What transfer?"

"Of you to Smith."

Again Sarah glared at the defence attorney and refused to answer. Again, Judge Armour told her to reply.

"Yes," she told the court. "A cow and a couple of dollars."

Two or three more female witnesses followed. Each revealed similar details about their personal lives. Finally, Judge Armour asked if these were the kind of witnesses the Crown intended to produce throughout the trial. "We take the witnesses just as they come," Macdougall stated.

"Well, I would not hang a dog on the testimony of such witnesses," Armour growled.[6]

The Crown did produce a few reliable witnesses, but none whose evidence was sufficient to convince the court that Joe Clemo was a killer. Clemo was set free, and the murder of Mr. Lowrie was officially unsolved.

Another Murder in Slabtown

Twenty-five years later, another murder in Slabtown made headlines. Again, the victim was an outsider.

In early May 1813, W.G. Wismer, A.C. Milne and Russell Becket were crossing the bridge over the Feeder Canal. Wismer noticed something strange in the water. One of the men used a pole to retrieve the object, which, to their horror, turned out to be a man's body.

A coroner's jury viewed the remains at J.A. Scholfield's funeral parlour. E.J. Aikens, C.M. Armstrong, John Bradford, W.M. Gray, W.R. Jackson J. Kelfer, A.G. McDowell, William Rogers, George H. Smith, J.F. Vanderburgh, George M. Watts and L. Werner learned that the man had been in his mid-twenties, about six feet tall, quite strong. He had been beaten severely and there was a serious wound at the base of the skull. However the autopsy, conducted by Dr. C.F. McVicar of

Toronto with the help of Dr. Charles Thrush of Dunnville, revealed that the man had drowned.

Decomposition had already begun, so it took a little while to identify the victim as Lorne Moss. An inquest opened on May 9 at the Dunnville Town Hall. Crown Attorney John Murphy, who had spent many years as Haldimand County's jailer before qualifying as a lawyer, examined witness after witness, and slowly pieced together information on Moss's final hours.

Lorne was a 25-year-old fisherman from Port Maitland who frequently took his boat into Dunnville. Although he was usually quiet and inoffensive, his character changed dramatically after a few drinks. Then he would get into fights. One such fight had occurred on the night of April 29 at Price's Hotel. According to testimony given by hotel owner James Price, who was tending bar that night, a wrestling match between Moss and George Noble had degenerated into a brawl. The next day, however, both men were drinking together, so apparently they had reconciled.

On May 1, Moss was seen by a number of people around Dunnville. Maggie Williams recalled seeing him around 8:30. Henry Williams saw him near the town hall about 9:30. Both of them, along with Ross Siddall and other witnesses, claimed that Lorne was worried about someone who was planning to beat him up. When he heard about this, Henry testified, he suggested that Lorne either walk back to Port Maitland or stay in town, rather than risk being ambushed when he returned to his boat. Lorne apparently replied that he would take whatever was coming to him. He appeared sober at the time. In fact, James Price testified that Moss had drunk no more than a few beers and the autopsy found no alcohol in his stomach.

After hearing all the witnesses, the jury came to the conclusion that "Lorne Moss came to his death by violence at the hands of some person or persons unknown."[7] The jury also recommended further investigation.

Soon official attention focused on one man, Jack Russell, who had recently become involved with Lorne's former girlfriend, Jennie Smith. Russell claimed he was away from Dunnville with two friends, George Price and Charles Weaver, on the night of Moss's death. But he behaved suspiciously when he learned Lorne's body had been found, leaving Dunnville abruptly.

As a result of the investigation, both Jack Russell and Jennie Smith were arrested. Although authorities lacked evidence to charge them with anything relating to the murder of Lorne Moss, they were both convicted of other offences. Jennie was sent to the Mercer Reformatory. Jack was sentenced to five years in Kingston penitentiary, but was given a suspended sentence provided he stay out of Dunnville. He quickly left town.

Meanwhile, the province put up a $500 reward for information leading to the arrest of Lorne's murderer. His brother, Edward Moss, added another $500. One thousand dollars was a substantial sum of money in 1913. But it was not enough to bring a murderer to justice. The man who killed Lorne Moss was never found.

The Killing of Mellie Sherk

When Ruby Sherk saw the front door to her uncle's house open, she knew something was wrong. It was early on the morning of March 3, 1947. Although her bachelor uncle, 72-year-old Joseph Melvin Sherk, was considered a bit strange by his Selkirk-area neighbours because of his reclusive ways, it was unlike him to leave a door ajar. So Ruby called her brother, Roy Sherk. Two neighbours, Albert and Ward Cook were also summoned and together they entered Mellie Sherk's house.

It was around 9 a.m. when they reached the bedroom. There they found the retired teacher slumped over the edge of his bed. He had been dead for some time.

The police were called in. Soon afterward, the investigation was turned over to Inspector T.R. Wright of the criminal investigation branch of the Ontario Provincial Police. Carefully, they pieced together the details of what had happened. Sometime in the middle of the night, one or more intruders had forced opened a window. Sherk was rumored to keep large quantities of cash in the house and, it was speculated, this was what had attracted the thief or thieves.

Apparently the intruders made enough noise to wake Sherk. Perhaps he called out. Perhaps he made a noise, which attracted the intruder. Whatever action he took, it proved to be fatal. Someone entered the room and shot him at close range. There was no sign of a struggle, suggesting the intruder may have been known to the elderly man.

Then the murder smashed open a safe, taking a quantity of cash and bonds. He also picked up a cash box which was later found shattered by the side of the road by one of Sherk's neighbours.

Heavy snowfall blocked many local roads, hampering the police investigation and covering any clues that might have led to a suspect. When Joseph Melvin Sherk was laid to rest in Selkirk's Union Cemetery, police were no closer to solving the case. There were rumors in the community about who may have committed the crime. In fact, the rumors persisted for years after Sherk's death. But no solid evidence was ever produced. The murder of Mellie Sherk was never solved.

Endnotes

Chapter One: The Notorious Townsend Gang

1. Messenger, Thomas. *The Lives, Trial, Confession and Execution of John Blowes & Geo. King*, 11.
2. McHenry, Robert J. *Narrative of the life of the daring murderer, highwayman & burglar, William Townsend*, 1.
3. *Cayuga Sachem*, 24 October 1854.
4. *Townsend: His Career and Trial at Cayuga*, 2.
5. Messenger, 5.
6. Messenger, 14.
7. Messenger, 13.
8. Messenger, 14.
9. Messenger, 10.
10. Messenger, 9.
11. "A Spectator" writing in the *Brantford Herald*; article reprinted in *The Globe*, 28 May 1855.
12. Messenger, 16.
13. Messenger, 13.
14. *Brantford Herald*, reprinted in *The Daily Spectator* (Hamilton), 24 May 1855.
15. Wallace, W. Stewart, *Murder and Mysteries*, 299.
16. Messenger, 4.
17. *Grand River Sachem*, 30 September 1857.
18. Messenger, 20.
19. *History of Welland County, Ontario*, 197.
20. *History of Welland County, Ontario*, 197.
21. Messenger, 18.
22. Messenger, 12.
23. Messenger, 24.

ChapterTwo: Haldimand County Courthouse

1 Haldimand County Council minutes, 28 January 1851, quoted in *Minutes and Auditor's Report of the County Council of the County of Haldimand for the Year 1950*, 168.

2. *Ibid*. February 25, 1851, 170.
3. *Haldimand Tribune*, 2 March 1865
4. *Ontario Sessional Papers:* "Annual Report of the Inspector of Asylums, Prisons, &c., for the Province of Ontario" 12 June 1884. Hereinafter "Prison report."
5. *Haldimand Advocate*, 28 December 1922.
6. *Hamilton Herald*, 22 September 1924.
7. *Hamilton Herald*, 22 September 1924.
8. *Haldimand Advocate*, 25 September 1924.

Chapter Three: Jailbreak! John and James Young

1. *The Confessions of John & James Wm. Young, the Murderers of the Late Abel McDonald of the Township of Walpole.* Caledonia: William T. Sawle, "Sachem" Office, 1876., 14. Hereinafter *Confessions.*
2. *Confessions* , 14.
3. *Confessions* , 9.
4. *Confessions* , 9.
5. *Confessions*, 10.

6. *Hamilton Evening Times,* quoted by Brian Henley in "'Foul' murder, escape, captivated Hamilton," *Hamilton Spectator,* 9 August 1997.
7. *Confessions*, 3.
8. From Sawle's (*Confessions*) account, it appears John and James Young made a verbal confession in the spring but it was not transcribed until later.
9. In his confession, James claims he used a boot, and that Lawrence remained conscious. However the 1877 report of the provincial inspector of prisons and a Hamilton *Spectator* article of 30 May 1876 indicate that James used the leg irons to beat Lawrence into unconsciousness.
10. *Daily Spectator*, 1 June 1876.
11. *Daily Spectator*, 14 June 1876.
12. *Daily Spectator*, 14 June 1876.
13. Prison Report, 1877.
14. *Daily Spectator*, 14 June 1876.
15. *Confessions* , 12.
16. Quoted by Brian Henley in "'Foul' murder, escape, captivated Hamilton," *Hamilton Spectator,* 9 August 1997.
17. *Confessions*, 5.
18. *Confessions*, 6.
19. *Confessions,* 6.
20. *Confessions*, 6.

Chapter Four: **Early Days at the County Jail**

1. Prison Report, 1872-3.
2.Prison Report, 1875, 94.
3. Prison Report, 1875, 94.
4. Prison Report, 1876.
5. Quoted in *Grand Heritage: A History of Dunnville and the Townships of Canborough, Dunn, Moulton, Sherbrooke and South Cayuga.* Dunnville: Dunnville District Heritage Association, 1992, 398.
6. Women were seldom sent to prison for debt because their ability to control money or enter into contracts which might lead to debt was severely limited by law.
7. Prison Report, 1880.
8. Prison Report for the year ending 31 October 1932. Total earnings from jail labour across the province was $2,522.63, with only three jails reporting: Kingston, Cayuga and Kenora.
9.*Haldimand Tribune,* 29 June 1865.
10. Prison Report, 1882.
11. "The Courthouses" by Monica Walsh. Typescript, *ca* 1937, Haldimand County Museum.
12. *Haldimand Tribune,* 15 December 1864.
13. *Haldimand Tribune,* 15 December 1864.
14. *Haldimand Tribune,* 2 March 1865
15."J." - to *Haldimand Tribune*, letter dated June 6, 1865
16. Prison Report, 1869.
17. Prison Report, 1872.
18. Prison Report, 1877.
19. Walsh.
20. Prison Report, 1878.
21. Prison Report, 1890.

Chapter Five: Sex and Scandal

1. "'Foul' murder, escape, captivated Hamilton" by Brian Henley in *The Hamilton Spectator*, 9 August 1997.
2. *Haldimand Advocate*
3. *Toronto Globe* quoted in "The Bloomsburg Tragedy" by Cheryl MacDonald in *Heritage Highlights: Stories from Haldimand and Norfolk*, Heronwood Writing Services: 1994, 3.
4. *Hamilton Spectator*, 14 October 1903.
5. *Hamilton Spectator*, 14 October 1903.
6. *Hamilton Spectator*, 14 October 1903.
7. *Hamilton Spectator*, 14 October 1903.
8. *Hamilton Spectator*, 14 October 1903.
9. *Hamilton Spectator*, 20 October 1903.
10. *Hamilton Spectator*, 20 October 1903.
11. *Hamilton Spectator*, 1 December 1903.
12. *Hamilton Spectator*, 1 December 1903.
13. *Hamilton Spectator*, 1 December 1903.
14. *Hamilton Spectator*, 1 December 1903.
15. *Hamilton Spectator*, 1 December 1903.
16. *Hamilton Spectator*, 1 December 1903.
17. *Hamilton Spectator*, 2 December 1903.

Chapter Six: Murder and Matrimony

1. *Grand River Sachem*, 22 July 1857.
2. *Grand River Sachem*, 22 July 1857.
3. *Grand River Sachem*, 29 July 1857.
4. *Grand River Sachem*, 29 July 1857.
5. *Brantford Expositor*, 11 December 1896.
6. *Brantford Expositor*, 11 December 1896.
7. *Brantford Expositor*, 11 December 1896.
8. *Brantford Expositor*, 14 December 1896.
9. *Brantford Expositor*, 14 December 1896.
10. *Brantford Expositor*, 14 December 1896.
11. *Brantford Expositor*, 14 December 1896.
12. A full account of the case can be found in *Who Killed George? The Ordeal of Olive Sternaman* by Cheryl MacDonald.
13. *Haldimand Advocate*, 26 June 1924.
14. *Haldimand Advocate*, 26 June 1924.
15. *Haldimand Advocate*, 26 June 1924.
16. Information relayed to Barbra Lang Walker, curator, Edinburgh Square, Caledonia, by George Gilbertson's niece, Isabel Gilbertson Hartwick.

Chapter Seven : Mrs. Perkins Goes to Trial

1. *Dunnville Chronicle*, 8 February 1907.
2. *Dunnville Chronicle*, 25 January 1907.
3. *Globe*, 20 April 1907.
4. *Dunnville Chronicle*, 25 January 1907.
5. *Dunnville Chronicle*, 15 February 1907.
6. *Globe*, 19 April 1907.
7. *Globe*, 8 March 1907.
8. *Globe*, 8 March 1907.
9. *Globe*, 8 March 1907.

10. The letter, which appeared in the Dunnville *Chronicle* on 22 March 1907 had already been published in the Cayuga *Advocate*.
11. *Dunnville Chronicle*, 19 April 1907.
12. *Globe*, 18 April 1907.
13. *Globe*, 20 April 1907.
14. *Globe*, 19 April 1907.
15. *Globe*, 19 April 1907.
16. *Globe*, 19 April 1907.
17. *Globe* - 24 April 1907

Chapter Eight: Justices, Judges and Others

1.Inscription on back of photo in Haldimand County Museum, Cayuga. The inscription was written by Catherine B. Rice, Taylor's granddaughter and possibly taken from Taylor's obituary.
2. *Haldimand Advocate*, 21 February 1907 .
3.*The Canadian Biographical Dictionary and Portrait Gallery of Eminent and Self-made Men*: Ontario volume, Toronto: American Biographical Publishing Company, 1880,, p. 252-3
4.*Simcoe Reformer*, 1 August 1929.
5. *Grand Heritage*, 248,
6. "Ladies of the Jury" by Svanhuit Josie in *Saturday Night*, 9 August 1952, 32.

Chapter Nine: Strange Crimes and An Unusual Punishment

1. *Jarvis Record*, 21 December 1910.
2. *Jarvis Record*, 28 December 1910.
3. *Haldimand Advocate*, 20 May 1920.
4. *Haldimand Advocate*, 27 May 1920.
5. *Haldimand Advocate*, 27 May 1920.
6. *Haldimand Advocate*, 10 June 1920.
7. *Haldimand Advocate*, 10 June 1920.
8. *Haldimand Advocate*, 10 June 1920.
9. Quoted in "Heritage Lane" by Cheryl MacDonald. Probably *Jarvis Record*.
10. Personal communication with Lynn Jaques.

Chapter Ten: Unsolved Murders

1. John Wilson Murray: *Memoirs of a Great Detective*. London: Heinemann, 1904, 271-272.
2. *Memoirs of a Great Detective*, 274.
3. *Memoirs of a Great Detective*, 277.
4. *Memoirs of a Great Detective*, 275.
5. *Memoirs of a Great Detective*, 276.
6. The account of the court testimony appears in *Memoirs of a Great Detective*, 276-277. However, it must be remembered that the memoirs were written long after the trial, probably by a journalist acting as Murray's ghostwriter. More than likely Murray or the ghostwriter exaggerated the story.
7. Quoted in *Grand Heritage*, 230.

Selected Bibliography

Books

Boyd, Neil. *The Last Dance: Murder in Canada*. Scarborough: Prentice Hall Canada Inc. 1988.

The Canadian Biographical Dictionary and Portrait Gallery of Eminent and Self-made Men: Ontario Volume. Toronto: American Biographical Publish Company, 1880.

Duff, Louis B. *The County Kerchief.* Toronto: Ryerson Press, 1949.

History of Welland County, Ontario. Welland: Welland Tribune Printing, 1887

Illustrated Historical Atlas of the Counties of Haldimand and Norfolk, 1877-1879 Toronto: H.R. Page and Company.

MacDonald, Cheryl (Ed.) *Grand Heritage: A History of Dunnville and the Townships of Canborough, Sherbrooke, Dunn, Moulton and South Cayuga*. Dunnville: Dunnville District Heritage Association, 1992.

----------------------. *Heritage Highlights: Stories from Haldimand and Norfolk*. Nanticoke: Heronwood Writing Services, 1994.

----------------------. *Who Killed George? The Ordeal of Olive Sternaman*. Toronto: Natural Heritage, Natural History Inc. 1994.

Martindale, Barbara. *Caledonia: Along the Grand River.* Toronto: Natural Heritage/Natural History Inc., 1995.

Murray, John Wilson. *Memoirs of a Great Detective*. London: Heinemann, 1904.

Wallace, W. Stewart, *Murder and Mysteries.* Toronto: The Macmillan Company of Canada Limited, 1931.

Government Reports

Auditor's Report of the County Council of the County of Haldimand for the Year 1950.

Ontario Sessional Papers

Periodicals and Pamphlets

Lethwaite, Susan, "Violence, Law and Community in Rural Upper Canada," in *Essays in the History of Canadian Law*, Vol. 5, Toronto: University of Toronto Press, 1981.

Josie, Svanhuit, "Ladies of the Jury" in *Saturday Night*, 9 August 1952.

Messenger, Thomas. *The Lives, Trial, Confession and Execution of John Blowes & Geo. King, Two of the Townsend Gang, Who Were Executed at Cayuga, C.W. on the 18th Day of May, 1855 for the Murder of John H. Nelles.* Buffalo: Thomas Messenger, 1855.

Sawle, William T. *The Confessions of John & James Wm. Young, the Murderers of the Late Abel McDonald of the Township of Walpole.* Caledonia: Sachem Office, 1876.

Newspapers

Brantford Expositor

Brantford Herald

Grand River Sachem

Haldimand Advocate

Haldimand Tribune

Hamilton Evening Times

Dunnville Chronicle

Hamilton Spectator

Norfolk Reformer

Norfolk Observer

Port Dover Maple Leaf

Simcoe Reformer

The Globe (Toronto)

Waterford Star

Other

Personal correspondence with Barbra Lang Walker, Edinburgh Square Heritage ane Cultural Centre, Caledonia.

Conversation with Lynn Jaques.

Personal files on Haldimand and Norfolk History

Miscellaneous files, Haldimand County Museum.

Photo Credits

Page 11 *The Lives, Trial, Confession and Execution of John Blows & Geo. King*
Page 15 *The Lives, Trial, Confession and Execution of John Blows & Geo. King*
Page 19 *Narrative of the life of the daring murderer, highwayman burglar, William Townsend.*
Page 23 National Archives of Canada.Cayuga Court House and Jail by James G. McKay, from *Canadian Illustrated News*, 23 September 1876.
Page 25 *Page's Illustrated Atlas.*
Page 26 Haldimand County Museum.
Page 27 Haldimand County Museum.
Page 30 Haldimand County Museum.
Page 31 Haldimand County Museum.
Page 36 Haldimand County Museum.
Page 41 Hamilton Public Library, Special Collections/ *Canadian Illustrated News,* August 28, 1876.
Page 52, 53, 55Cheryl MacDonald.
Page 73 *Memoirs of A Great Detective.*
Page 76 Cheryl MacDonald.
Page 82 Haldimand County Museum.
Page 87 Allison Gowling.
Page 89 Haldimand County Museum.
Page 92 Haldimand County Museum.
Page 93 Haldimand County Museum.
Page 94 Haldimand County Museum.
Page 95 Haldimand County Museum.
Page 97 Haldimand County Museum.
Page 98 Haldimand County Museum.
Page 99 Haldimand County Museum.
Page 103 Haldimand County Museum.
Page 108 Dunnville District Heritage Association.

Personal Names Index

General Index

-L-

-M-

-N-

-O-

-P-

-R-

-S-

-T-

-U-

-W-

-Y-

About the Author

Cheryl MacDonald has been writing about Haldimand County since 1980. A longtime resident of Nanticoke, she is a professional writer and historian whose weekly history column has appeared in the *Simcoe Times-Reformer* since the mid-1980s. Her previously published books include *Niagara Daredevils, Great Canadian Love Stories, Who Killed George?, Port Dover: A Summer Garden* and *Chronicle of Canada.* Cheryl is a professional member of the Periodical Writers Association of Canada and the Canadian Authors Association.

Haldimand History: Crime and Punishment, 1850-1950 is the second title in a six-part series on Haldimand County.